THE SILENT HEROES

A Memoir of Holland During World War II

By
Hans Moederzoon van Kuilenburg

Strategic Book Publishing and Rights Co.

Back cover photo by Barbara Winters
Front cover photo by the author

Strategic Book Publishing and Rights Co.
12620 FM 1960, Suite A4-507
Houston, TX 77065
www.sbpra.com

ISBN: 978-1-62212-281-3

Book Design: Suzanne Kelly

Acknowledgements

With the greatest thanks to my friend Rose Anne Wright Goacher for her help in getting this work together. Rosy, I owe you!

Matt and Tina Thompson, many thanks to you both for your encouragement and the faith you had in me that I would finally do it. Tina, thank you for practically forcing me to write this book!

With deep gratitude and thanks to Barbara Winters, my friend and editor.

My children Roy and Manon for their endless patience helping me with computer problems, after all when I was born there were no computers. Hans and Nicole for always supporting all I do.

Foreword

By Tina Thompson

If we are fortunate throughout our lives, we have a handful of special people that inspire, motivate, intrigue, and connect with us in irreplaceable ways. When we speak with these extraordinary friends, we feel alive, astute, stimulated, and we sense mutual admiration. We look forward to our times spent with these individuals, because we know we will laugh, learn, and sometimes agonize with them. More than that, we know we will be in the company of a loved one with whom we share a mutual admiration. These friends sometimes come from vastly different walks of life, and perhaps much of the pleasure we feel for them is the fascination we hold for their stories.

Hans van Kuilenburg is such a friend. The story of her life growing up in German-occupied Holland during World War II is one that is fascinating. The sacrifices her family and contemporaries made are inconceivable to me, as someone who grew up in a comfortable and protected life in the mid-western United States. Our relationship actually began with Hans being introduced to our family by my husband, after becoming acquainted with each other at work. He has always had an acute perception of positive personality and is drawn to intriguing individuals. As such, I met our dear friend, Hans. Our friendship has grown into somewhat of a mother-child relationship, as I now often consult her wealth of knowledge and life experiences. My family truly loves Hans. My children think of her as a grandmotherly figure. My parents have enjoyed conversations with her, and I feel a sense of sibling affection for her children.

Hans has the remarkable ability to remember minute details. She has captivated many dinner-party guests with stories from her childhood. They come out as matter-of-fact accounts of life as it was for everyone in Holland during that time. In fact, it is true that Hans' success in life can be attributed to her early life experiences, hard work, strong will, and determination. Not only is she an alluring story-teller, she is also quite an accomplished cook and former restaurateur. So an invitation to Hans' house for dinner is one full of promises of good food, good friends, and good conversation.

Late in life, Hans realized, quite accidentally, that she has a remarkable gift for photography. After friends began urging her to display and sell her photographs, largely landscapes, she has held many exhibits and has developed a successful, web-based art business. This has proven to be a daunting, yet gratifying, learning experience for Hans. Along with the undertaking of building the photography entrepreneurship, have come several trips to Europe. There, Hans has had the pleasure of connecting with long-lost friends and much-missed family members, as she has traveled back to her roots, taking many beautiful landscape and historical photographs, and recollecting the stories of her childhood, many of which are quite traumatic.

Yet these stories are ones that must be told. They must be told so that generations to come may understand the atrocities that have occurred throughout history. They must be told so that we may know of the survival instincts these victims of violence have bravely displayed. These stories must be told so that we not forget, in order that we not repeat the brutality of the past. Thank goodness for the special people in our lives, those who touch a chord with us, share with us, inspire us, and teach us the goodness and endurance of human nature. Thank you, Hans, for sharing the story of your childhood with us.

Table of Contents

THE SILENT HEROES

Dedicated to Peace on Earth

Introduction

Through the years, many friends have urged me to write down my memories of occupied Netherlands during World War II.

I grew up in Amsterdam, then a city of about 900,000, plus another 100,000 or so in the suburbs. Almost ten percent of the population was comprised of Jews. The law office where my father worked for many years was directly across the canal from the business office owned by Otto Frank, father of Anne Frank. While I did not know Anne, my father and Mr. Frank greeted each other from a distance on many a morning on their way to work, one could say like friendly acquaintances.

I have started this project many times, but found it difficult after so many years. While recording these memories, I re-lived many horrific events of the war years, and found myself many times breaking down into tears. In any event, these are my memories—those of a Dutch woman, now in my eighties, recalling my adolescence and five miserable years of oppression which changed my life forever.

CHAPTER 1

The Family

My paternal grandparents were Hermanus and Klasina Erb Moederzoon. Hermanus worked for the power company, and Klasina was a housewife. My father, Willem-Frederik—'Wim'—was one of nine children; only seven, however, survived to adulthood.

My maternal grandparents were Otto-Hendrik and Johanna—'Anna'—Cornelia Groen Röckener. Otto held a job as a civilian for the Dutch Army, and Anna was a housewife. My mother, Ria, short for Hendrika-Petronella, was one of four children, three girls and a boy. The boy, who was my uncle, was the youngest. He was named Otto after his father. My mother was extremely pretty, and the apple of her father's eye. I am told this created tension, and perhaps a bit of jealousy, between my mom and her mother.

I am the eldest child in my family. My given name is Hendrika Wilhelmina—'Hans'—followed by a sister, Wilhelmina-Hendrika—'Willy.' My parents did not have a lot of imagination, did they? My brothers, Frederik-Peter—'Fred'—and Johan-Christian-Hendrik—'John'—are five and ten years younger than I am, respectively. Fred and I share the same birthday, making him exactly five years younger than I am. Since I am one of four children, as was my mother, and am also the parent of four, I have felt that four is the magic number for our family. It is good to believe in something magical.

CHAPTER 2

Prelude to War

Much has been written about World War II by generals, statesmen, historians and the like. For the most part, I have written from the perspective of my memories and thoughts about the war. I am now an older woman looking back on my life during World War II, from my home in the United States, more than sixty-five years later.

It was indeed a war of global proportions, with fronts in Europe and the Orient. I can understand that many may know little about the role of the Netherlands, a small country—about one-fifth the size of Michigan where I now live—in this enormous war. However, I feel this deserves to be better known. I have learned that we suffered more German brutality than any of the other occupied countries. As such, I have supplemented my personal recollections with information gathered from research. Included is a look at how and why this war happened, and why Germany was not stopped—as they should have been—after World War I.

Historians agree that the outcomes of World War I were important factors in the development of World War II. I'll begin with a brief look at the onset and impact of The Great War, as World War I was called in my youth.

Until the eighteenth century, armies were comprised mostly of volunteers. Frequently, soldiers also were for hire. Think of the Prussians, Hessians, Bavarians and Saxons who fought on American soil. All of these men were from some part of Germany, and warriors to the max. Ordinary people were foot soldiers, and the so-called upper classes became officers. The militarization of Europe in the nineteenth century brought forth the conscription (draft) of young men. Military service became popular, because it was an experience of equality. The thought at the time was that every male citizen should be a soldier, as each soldier also was a citizen, and so that seemed to have made sense. Therefore, my grandfather Otto was drafted as a young man and served in the military for two years; luckily he was not in any war. I never heard if my paternal grandfather was drafted, likely not, for he was severely asthmatic.

Compared to the nationalistic revolutions before it, World War I was a global conflict. The Allied Powers were France, the Russian Empire, the British Empire, the Empire of Japan; and later Italy and the United States. The Central Powers were the German Empire (Second Reich), Austria, Hungary, Bulgaria, and the Ottoman (Turkish) Empire.

Compare this to World War II, which involved sixty-one countries. The most visible change was Japan moving from ally in the first war to enemy in the second. In addition, Russia/USSR changed sides several times from World War I to early World War II, before firmly ending up in the Allied camp. And how bravely those Russians fought; it looked so hopeless for them at the onset, but the tide turned. It was said that Hitler's greatest mistake was to fire his field marshals and take over the command himself as it became his undoing. He had experience as a corporal, but certainly not as a general.

Although sparked by the assassination of the heir to the Austrian throne in June 1914, the ultimate causes of World War I were multiple and complex. Among them was a climate of military elitism, economic imperialism, military preparedness—the naval arms race between Britain and Germany—and last but not least, Germany's war plans against France and Russia. This left Germany anxious to seize the initiative for decisive victories. Twenty million European youths took up arms in World War I. There were enormous losses on all sides, and by the time the fighting ended in November 1918, the toll for both sides was ten million military dead, twenty million injured and eight million missing.

3

In optimism, The Great War was called "the war to make the world safe for democracy," and "the war to end all wars." To ensure this would be true, the Allied leaders took steps to prevent Germany from being able to ever again fight such a war. So then how was it possible that Germany was able to gain the military strength for World War II, given the restrictions imposed on them after The Great War?

The signing of the peace treaty of World War I took place at the Palace of Versailles on June 28, 1919. It was one of Germany's blackest hours, as they were forced to face responsibility for starting the previous four years of bloodshed. They lost their overseas empire and they were virtually disarmed. They were prohibited from having any tanks or airplanes, and the once six-million-man army was slashed to 100,000 volunteers.

To supplement the meager official army, the Germans responded by starting a volunteer rifle corps. These so-called free-corps ("frei-corps") sprung up all over the country. However, this was small potatoes compared to what was going on away from the public eye.

Before the ink had dried on the Treaty of Versailles, a cagey old general, Hans von Seeckt, was setting in motion a series of clandestine events designed to lead to the rebirth of the German military and industrial might. As the commander of the Reichswehr (German Army), von Seeckt began conspiring to use the authorized 100,000-man force as a cadre for future rapid expansion. Only the best-educated officers and sergeants, who had proven themselves to be dynamic leaders and courageous in battle, were allowed to remain in this service.

Many British and American officers were stationed throughout Germany to make certain the terms of the peace treaty were enforced. So von Seeckt and his army co-conspirators had to proceed with extreme caution and utilize ingenious deceptions to mask what was really taking place.

Once von Seeckt had selected the members of his private club, he made certain that their living conditions were vastly improved. They had food items not available to civilians, and their pay was increased. General von Seeckt then established a strict routine of sports and other recreational activities aimed at developing strong, healthy soldiers.

von Seeckt next created a series of military schools whose "civilian" instructors were in reality high-ranking officers from The Great War, who taught sergeants and lieutenants the techniques of commanding entire divisions, in preparation for some future war. Among the eager students was young Erwin Rommel, a platoon leader in The Great War, whose superiors had already identified him as being not only tireless and brave, but also cunning to the point of ruthlessness, traits he would become famous for in the upcoming war.

In 1921, without informing the German government, von Seeckt brokered a clandestine mutual assistance pact with Vladimir (Nicolai) Lenin of the Soviet Union, against whom Germany fought so bitterly in The Great War. The alliance was instigated by Lenin, whose country's economy—like that of Germany—was plagued by runaway inflation. It was a marriage born of necessity. The Red Army lacked both professional leadership skills and military schools for training; Germany had no tanks, airplanes or heavy guns, no air force or navy. The alliance certainly looked like a win-win situation, and they never imagined that each was strengthening its future enemy.

Under the terms of the pact, German military advisers secretly assisted the Soviet Union in modernizing its army. In return, the German army would receive periodic clandestine shipments of Soviet-built heavy weapons. The best of the German army were sent—in civilian clothes—to the Soviet Union to be trained on the planes and tanks being developed there by German armament experts.

Each year, a third of the annual budget of the German army went to a curious cartel known as The Industrial Enterprises Development Corporation. From its offices, one in Berlin and one in Moscow, it dealt directly with the Soviet government, and had several subcontracting branches throughout the Soviet Union. This seemingly commercial corporation was a cover for re-armament.

Under the direction of the bogus firm, aircraft shells, submarines and poison gas were produced in the Soviet Union and covertly shipped to Germany. This was done right under the noses of the British, French, and Americans stationed in Germany to ensure that the peace treaty was enforced. What on earth were they doing—sleeping? Certainly not their job!

In September 1921, at his headquarters in Berlin, General von Seeckt set up Sundergraeppe R (Special Group R), the cover name for an operation run by selected officers to coordinate the numerous secret manufacturing and military assistance programs taking place in the Soviet Union. At the same time, von Seeckt dispatched one of his key officers, Colonel Oscar von Niedermayer, to the Soviet Union to open Zentrale Moskau (Moscow Central). He immediately began dashing about Russia in civilian clothes, carrying orders to coordinate all secret German activities in that country. He gave special attention to three immense training bases in very remote parts of the Soviet Union that were being prepared to conduct extensive and realistic field exercises for the Schwartze Reichswehr—the German "Black Army."

These 20,000 soldiers were the best and the brightest, destined for high command in some future German army. At the camps, high-ranking German officers taught the art of war to both the men of the Black Army and to young Soviet officers also selected for future high command in their own army.

One finds many things named "black" in this time. It is used to mean operating contrary to public regulation, as in "the black market." The Black Army was sent to training camps under the most stringent secrecy. Before leaving Germany, all names were "erased" from the rolls, so theoretically none of them actually existed. The rigorous training exercises sometimes used live ammunition; some deaths were inevitable. To preserve the secrecy, hermetically sealed zinc containers were used to bring back the remains of German soldiers killed in training.

Another area in which Germany re-armed was her air force. Although the 1919 Treaty of Versailles had directed that Germany destroy all of its combat aircraft, and prohibited them from building more of them, the document unfortunately made no mention of the use of glider planes.

Almost immediately, scores of active glider clubs sprang up throughout Germany, and glider flying became a craze during the first years after World War I. A lot of young pilots looked upon their flying as an enjoyable pastime and sport. Many others envisioned the clubs as excellent training grounds for flying power planes, and the time when Germany would again have an air force.

One of the latter was Hermann Goering, who at the time was employed as a salesman. During The Great War, Goering had been a highly-decorated fighter ace, with no less than twenty kills. Indeed, after the notorious Red Baron (Manfred von Richthofen) was shot down, Goering took over as squadron leader. As a civilian in an intolerable post-war Germany, he was very bitter about the Treaty of Versailles, and vowed revenge.

In early 1922, Captain Edward Rickenbacker, America's top fighter pilot in The Great War, then a top executive with an aviation corporation, was in Berlin on business. Four former German pilots played host to him, one of them being Goering. During a conversation at dinner, Goering apparently described to the American how Germany would recapture its empire through air power.

One can imagine Rickenbacker's shock. Only four years after the greatest butchery in history had ended, here was a famous pilot from the butcher's army, advocating rebuilding the nation's armed might and going to war once again. One has to wonder if the men had too much to drink with dinner, because Goering told his former American enemy precisely how Germany would circumvent the restrictions of the Treaty of Versailles. He described the three-fold plan: first to promote gliding as a sport to young men, second to build up commercial aviation, and finally to create the skeleton of a military air force, pulling together all three factors when the time was right.

Indeed, early in 1923 the rules of the Treaty were somewhat relaxed, including permission to build a limited number of civilian airplanes. Not surprisingly, the German aircraft manufacturers gave a liberal interpretation to "limited number," and produced many "civilian" aircraft, in all sizes.

In circumvention of more rules, von Seeckt proceeded with his master plan to re-arm Germany by creating an illegal "Schwartze Luftwaffe" (Black Air Force)—a special aviation branch—and the Flugerzentrale (Flying Center) was formed with a few squadrons of aircraft converted from civilian use.

Modern aviation equipment and design were sorely lacking, due to the Treaty restrictions. So scouts were sent out to foreign countries to purchase items that were readily available on the open market. Efforts focused on the United States, although they soon learned that a lot of the things the scouts sought were classified military secrets by the War Department in Washington. So what couldn't be bought would often be stolen.

The task of pilfering U.S. military secrets was handed to Abwehr, Germany's equivalent of the Secret Service, which sent Wilhelm Lonkowski to do the job. His passport identified him as William Schneider, a piano tuner. He had been furnished with a shopping list. This lone agent was expected to steal secrets from Curtis Aircraft, Westinghouse, Seversky Aviation, Fairchild Aviation and Douglas Aircraft, as well as the army's Mitchell and Roosevelt airfields outside New York City. Lonkowski quickly determined that the United States was a spy's paradise. There was no Department of Homeland Security as we have today. Indeed, at that time, the United States was the only major nation in the world that had no service to ferret out and protect against the intentions of hostile powers. Consequently, unhindered by fear of detection or arrest, Lonkowski rapidly recruited a network of domestic spies, and began reaping a harvest of America's military secrets.

Meanwhile, back in Germany, von Seeckt was busy organizing another ruse to expand the Army's clout. Devising an intentionally misleading name, he created the Gruppenamt (simply, The Group), consisting of sixty of his most capable officers. For all practical purposes, it was a new general staff.

Von Seeckt also used evasive means to make sure that Germany would have a large pool of highly trained reserve officers. He achieved that goal by rotating men through the Army, keeping its strength at 100,000 at any given time, while training more than an additional 100,000.

Thus by the early 1930s, when new leader Adolf Hitler told the world that Germany was no longer bound by the Treaty of Versailles, and began rapidly and overtly to expand its armed forces, Germany already had a large, motivated, and highly skilled officers corps—perhaps the best in the world. They now had trained soldiers and fighter pilots, and a significant quantity of planes and modern military armament.

CHAPTER 3

Early Family Life

Whatever life handed them through the years, my parents shared a strong sense of adventure. The story of how they met reveals that spirit. It was 1926. My mother was a clerk in a grocery store where my father, a law office clerk, frequently shopped. Soon, he was stopping in daily to sometimes buy a single candy bar. He managed to be waited on only by my mother. She was twenty years old, and probably would not have paid him any attention if she had known he was only seventeen.

However, he kept that fact from her, and when he eventually brought up the idea of going on a date together, she accepted and suggested ice skating. My dad quickly agreed, even though he had never skated before in his life. My mother probably suspected this when he showed up wearing a long winter coat and a bowler hat. Those suspicions were quickly confirmed when he couldn't stay on his feet on the ice; but she liked his spirit. That was both the first and the last time that my father ever skated, yet it was a great beginning to their courtship.

My parents were married in 1929, the year of the beginning of the Great Depression. My father was just twenty-one when I was born the following year; my mom was twenty-three. They moved in with my maternal grandparents for about three years, to save money so they could afford their own place. It was difficult, a challenge, in such hard times. To complicate matters, I was born with a disability; my kneecap was on the inside of my left leg. I now know that it is an inherited birth defect, for I have a second cousin who had this same condition, though we were not aware of this at that time.

When I was born, the doctor and nurse told my mother that there was something wrong with her baby. They did not say what was wrong at first, but mom was insistent to find out. So they unwrapped the clothing from around me and showed her my leg, with the kneecap on the inside of my leg. She let out a scream, believing that her first child would never walk. But over time I did, surprising everyone, though the work and effort of a good doctor.

When I was six weeks old, my mother took me to the clinic where they were going to check my little leg. She had yet another fright. We were in the midst of a construction zone where loose planks were stacked. Kids were running around and caused some of the planks to fall, hitting me on my head. This resulted in the early closing of the soft part of my head—the fontanel—which knitted itself together at once. It remained a bump on my skull. Fortunately, my hair is covering the remnants of the injury, which could have been so much worse. Still, it remains a reminder of that day.

On top of all this, my mother remained overly cautious about my leg and I never did learn how to fall properly, like other children. Not that I really would like to fall, I don't think any one does, but I have a hunch that it would be a real trauma. Although the knee was quickly taken care of, and I was able to walk, my father still carried me everywhere. My mother worried constantly that I would fall, and that any progress would become undone, for this is what she had been told.

The Depression did not affect us too much, since my family had steady employment. My father had his job at the law office. He once held the record as the fastest typist in the Netherlands. He switched jobs when my Grandfather Otto told him of a job opening as an office clerk with the Dutch Marines. Just before the war began, he was promoted to manager of marine supplies, which included food and clothing, an achievement we were all happy about. I now had two family members working for the government—my grandfather and my father.

My early youth was quite normal. My mother was a house-wife, a practical role at the time. In addition to the usual cooking and cleaning, (she had purchased a Singer sewing machine when she was nineteen years old), she sewed and mended and kept us looking nice. She also had many other skills and eventually owned and operated her own business, but more about that later.

I remember playing train with my Grandfather Otto, by putting chairs in a row in a hallway with all the doors closed. My aunt, who was just sixteen when she began to date my uncle, was a member of the family by this time. She remembered, "We all had to do what you said, and pretend we were riding in a train." What a bossy little thing I must have seemed!

I adored my Grandfather Otto. At age four, I had a tonsillectomy. While in the hospital, only my parents could visit. Grandfather Otto was not allowed to come in, probably due to fear of infection—or so I thought. He stood outside my room for the longest time, waving and throwing me kisses. I have never forgotten that image. There was one day when he stood outside my window for hours.

By the time I came home from the hospital, my grandfather had died. Unbeknownst to me, while I was in the hospital, he too had been hospitalized. He went in to have a simple, routine hernia repair, developed a blood clot, and died as a result.

Although nothing could replace my dear Grandfather Otto, there was a gift from my grandparents for me when I came home. It was a little tea set which I have to this day. He must have helped to pick out the gift for me before he went into the hospital.

His death devastated my mother; she cried for days on end. I, too, loved and missed him very much and often felt I needed him desperately, thought I frequently felt he was near me—a lovely gift of my vivid imagination. How I have missed him, longing for his love and kindness, when things got rough through the years.

Shortly before my fifth birthday, I entered kindergarten and promptly got the typical childhood diseases, including whooping cough, measles, mumps, and chicken pox. Being a generous child, I shared these all with my brother and sister. I liked kindergarten and went from 9 a.m. to noon and again from 2 p.m. to 4 p.m. We went home for lunch during the break. For me, that was only a five minute walk. Mom would always be there with lunch ready and then I would play. I never took naps. To this day, I have never been a 'nap person.' Back at school, we sang, played games, drew pictures, and colored—just like my children did when they were growing up. My mother also cooked dinner for the family every day.

I went on to grade school in 1937. Classes were large, about fifty students. I was eager to learn. I remember walking home through the park, most times with a girlfriend. By the time I was in third grade, in 1939, we had moved to the south side of Amsterdam. It was too far for me to come home for lunch. We had no idea at the time, but we had moved just before the start of the war.

The surname of the Dutch royal family is Oranje (Orange). The earliest Oranje I knew of existed around the mid-sixteenth century. There was an Earl in France with the surname d'Orange. When that Earl died childless, the title went to his cousin Willem in Germany, whose surname was van Nassau and who then became Willem van Oranje-Nassau, a name carried by the Royal family to this day. He was born in 1533 and died in 1584. His nickname was Willem de Zwijger (Willem the Silent). Willem de Silent was protestant, as is the Royal family today. Willem I Frederik, known as the Prince of Oranje, was born in 1772. Years later, after he married Mary Stuart, an Irish woman, he was invited by the Irish parliament to become their prince.

The Queen, at the time of my childhood, was Wilhelmina. She was the grandmother of the current Queen Beatrix. Her only child, Princess Juliana, married Prince Bernhard von Lippe Biesterveldt in 1937. The young couple made a visit to Amsterdam, and being a member of the Oranje Club, I had the honor and duty to curtsy and offer them flowers. I was about seven years old at the time, and never forgot Princess Juliana.

The Oranje Club was merely an after school activity to keep the children off of the streets. The tradition has become for many to don orange-colored garb at events such as the Olympics and soccer games. Princess Juliana was very kind, and remained so throughout her life. I later learned she had wanted to be a social worker, and I am sure she would have been a great one. Instead, she had no choice but to become the Queen when Wilhelmina abdicated in 1948.

Life plodded on. Until about age ten or eleven, I played with dolls. I had a doll house, and a kitchen. Eventually, my brother Freddy and my cousin Otto ruined my doll's kitchen by peeing in the pans. The smell was unbearable. I was very upset at them for this and threw all the pans away. Boys!!!

As a young girl, I went to the library a lot, and was very proud to have a book case of my own in my bedroom. I went to school and was a member of a youth theater and a ballet group. Despite starting life with a bad leg, I loved ballet and was considered a skilled dancer, even as a child.

Some other memories of my early years included The World Jamboree coming to the Netherlands in 1937. Because of this being held in Amsterdam, they built hundreds of new apartments for the people who came from all over the world to attend this worldwide Boy Scout event. I enjoyed listening to the music on the radio. I was only seven at the time, but I can still remember—and sing—the song from the Jamboree as we heard it constantly on the radio.

In 1939, the year my youngest brother, John, was born, we moved from the east of the city to the south, where we lived during the war and occupation. Additionally, my brother was born prematurely and required a lot of extra care. Also that year, I developed a middle-ear infection, which turned into encephalitis. I was gravely ill and nearly died. Our doctor, a Jewish man, made a house visit which was common back then. He told my mother if I made it through the night, I would be all right.

We had not yet heard of antibiotics; they did not come along until the 1940s. I do recall family members crying because they all thought I would be leaving them at too young an age. But it was not my time, for I am still here, more than three quarters of a century later. I recovered from the encephalitis and resumed the life of a young, adventurous girl. I returned to school and life proceeded almost as it had before I was taken ill.

Back in school, much to our disappointment, we did not have formal music instruction; rather, we had an hour of singing twice a week. That was as far as it went. In addition, girls had two hours of handicrafts, such as knitting and sewing, while the boys got to do some drawing. At that time, we girls were just expected to grow up to be housewives; as such, we needed to learn these skills. I remember knitting a sock without seams, the pour soul that would have to wear those, they were plank like. Since we still had a strong interest in music, my sister and I took piano lessons from 'Aunt Mary,' whose husband was a journalist of Jewish descent. We called him 'Uncle Max.' They were not blood relatives; however, as a sign of respect, growing up then in the Netherlands, children would often call their parents' friends 'aunt' and 'uncle.'

When I was around eight years old, my mom took my sister and me to see Shirley Temple in the film "On the Good Ship Lollypop." This was a big event as there was no television. Later, around 1940, my parents went to a ball; my father wore a curly wig and a dress with a layer of ruffles, playing Shirley Temple. I will never forget the sight of his milky white legs— my dad in a dress.

In the neighborhood where we lived, there were stores on each side of the street, as far as the eye could see. Apartments were built above them, usually three stories in addition to the businesses. We lived above a butcher shop, flanked by a grocery store to the right, and a bookstore on the left. Across the street were two stores owned by Jews: a large store that sold clothing and linens owned by the Roegs and next to that was a Jewish bakery and pastry shop.

The butcher shop was on the ground floor. Above it were apartments on the first, second, and third floors. We lived in the top apartment, on the third floor. We climbed four flights of stairs, each consisting of seventeen steps. Despite coming into the world with a cockeyed knee, the flights of stairs never bothered me. My boundless childhood energy took me up and down effortlessly.

The building was not very wide across the front, but each apartment ran deep back from the street. From the stairway, our apartment opened into an enclosed front hall. From the front hall, there were doors on the left to the bathroom and to the kitchen behind it. On the right, there was a door to a small front bedroom that Grandma Anna had moved into just before the war began. There was yet another door to the living room.

The living room was the full width of the building, behind the front rooms. At the far end of the living room, sliding wood doors led into a smaller room, the bedroom for my two brothers. At the far end of their bedroom, sliding wood doors led into a larger room, which was my parents' bedroom. At the far end of their room were double glass doors opening out to a balcony, where my mother grew red geraniums.

Up front was another flight of stairs to the attic, where each apartment had a somewhat enclosed, latticed section, to store coal and other items, as well as an extra bedroom. In our attic was the bedroom where my sister and I slept. We had a swing set there as well. It may sound like tight quarters for enjoying a swing, but if we opened the double window at the end, we could swing so high our feet would go out the window. We particularly loved to swing as high as possible.

We were one house from the corner of the street which housed the Asscher Diamond Factory, which was surrounded by a high fence for necessary security. It was the largest of its kind in Amsterdam, and perhaps anywhere at the time. It had an international reputation. The Asscher Brothers were requested by King Edward VII to cut the world's largest diamond—the Cullinan— and the two largest gems were then set in the Crown Jewels. There were always dignitaries coming to visit.

When we moved we did not change schools, but walked to the same one as before. We carried our lunch. There was only one other child, a boy, who stayed at lunchtime regularly; he lived in one of the canal houses, a lot fancier then our home. Our lunch period was two hours, from noon until 2 p.m. We played at the Oosterpark (East Park) which virtually adjoined the school.

I had my first boyfriend in the fourth grade. He traded me for a nickel to another boy. It does not sound like much, but we could buy candy for a penny. As backward as this may seem now, back then, I was in demand!

During the 1940s, my mother realized how much she liked to act, and became heavily involved in the theater. She was one of the theater leaders, a role that she enjoyed immensely. She was good at it, and soon developed quite a comedy routine.

Top: My identy papers.
Right: Opa Otto in the service.
Bottom: My second ration card.

Top, left: Opa Otto; right: Oma Anne.
Bottom: The entire Moederzoon Clan, the little boy with the enormous bow on the front left is my dad age 6.

Top: It is customary in Nederland to celebrate 12 1/2 year of marriage. The four of us kids and my parents at the party.
Middle: My sister and I in school, around 1942.
Bottom: The author at 16 years old.

Top right: My father.
Left: The four Moederzoon
children.
Bottom right: My mother,
Ria.

CHAPTER 4

The Rise of Hitler

The Germans were militarily prepared to launch World War II. That still leaves the question, why would they allow Adolph Hitler to lead them to war?

The countries to which World War I brought victory were mainly France and Britain. The war, though costly in loss of life, had improved their home economies. Their empires had enlarged, as some parts of Germany and its colonies had been given to Britain, France and some of the smaller players such as Turkey and Japan.

Stripped of tanks and airplanes, Germany could have no more than a 100,000-man army. Without real military force, a country cannot validate and protect its statehood, and these measures stung the proud Germans. In 1920, Germany was also ordered to begin paying $33 billion for war reparations, which immediately caused ruinous inflation.

Along came Adolph Hitler, asking for vengeance against the German punishments for World War I, and finding ever larger audiences for his message. He began his political career in 1920 with the National Socialist German Worker's Party (Nationsozialistische Deutsche Arbeiterpartei, (workers party) or NDSP, called Nazi for short.

In 1921, Hitler formed a private army called the Sturm Abteilung (SA or Storm Section). Also known as Storm Troopers or Brown Shirts, their missions were to disrupt meetings of political opponents and to protect Hitler from revenge attacks. The SA was a volunteer militia, with Hitler as its leader, and it soon numbered over 15,000.

In 1923, they attempted to overthrow the young democratic government in Berlin, but failed. Hitler was convicted of treason for his role in the attempted Nazi revolution, but the trial gave him an effective public platform for his ideas, and his sentence was light. During his nine months in prison, he dictated his book, *Mein Kampf*, promoting the supremacy of Germanic people and the inferiority of Jews and Russians among others. But the economy was improving and the citizenry contented. So from 1926 to 1929, the Nazi party bided its time. It quietly organized and prepared to overthrow the German democratic republic, and even developed its own government-in-waiting.

Beginning in 1929, the worldwide economic Depression destroyed credit throughout Europe. This economic crisis provided Hitler with new opportunities. Companies went bankrupt, banks failed, and people instantly lost life savings. Germany was especially vulnerable, as its economy was built on foreign capital, and loans were being called in. Poverty and starvation were very real possibilities for everyone.

In the election of 1930, the Nazi party polled eighteen percent—a startling leap from being the smallest to the second largest party in the country. In 1932, it won thirty-seven percent of the votes, with party membership at over a million. The SA militia now numbered 400,000, up from 15,000 just a few years earlier. Unemployment in this nation of eighty million was rampant and rose to six million, almost ten percent of the work force, by 1932.

Hitler was a very shrewd, calculating, manipulative, brawling psychopath, who relentlessly pursued his path to absolute power. Initially he appeared to work within the free election system, skillfully convincing voters, but also relying on political arm-twisting. He finally achieved the position of chancellor on January 30, 1933; but he wasn't stopping there. By March 23, his SA had violently crushed any opposition, rendering the democratic republic impotent, and he effectively became dictator. However, Germany retained a figurehead president, Raul von Hindenburg. On August 2, 1934, the 87-year-old died at his estate in East Prussia. Earlier, Hitler had obtained a political testament from a senile von Hindenburg, naming Hitler as his successor.

Hitler moved swiftly. He had no interest in merely being president. Only minutes after von Hindenburg died, Hitler proclaimed himself Führer—supreme leader—and launched a strategy to induce his admirals and generals to swear allegiance to him. No doubt acting on the Führer's orders, war minister von Blomberg directed all three hundred generals to assemble at 3 p.m. that same afternoon, at the foot of the Siegessaule, the towering Column of Victory in Berlin.

Unbeknownst to the high brass, Hitler was preparing a coup d'état that would give him total control of Germany and the armed forces. The generals had been told that they were to participate in ceremonies to honor the dead President von Hindenburg. Cannons were fired. A band played mournful tunes. There were two minutes of silence.

Then General von Blomberg stepped forward to take the Fahneneid, the Blood Oath of the Teutonic Knights. The army commander, General Werner von Fritsch, and General Ludwig Beck, followed. Each held the flag of Germany in one hand and the Bible in the other while reciting: "I swear by God this holy oath, that I will render to Adolph Hitler, Führer of the German nation and people, supreme commander of the armed forces, unconditional obedience, and I am ready as a soldier to risk my life at any time for this oath." All over Germany, at the same time, the rank and file of the armed forces recited the same blood oath.

According to Generals von Fritsch and Beck, as soon as it was over they realized that they had been hoodwinked into swearing a completely new form of the oath, not to Germany or to the constitution, but to Adolph Hitler. They considered it a fateful turning point, one which meant physical and moral suicide. But whatever their shock and regret, they did not dare to forsake the oath.

Next, Hitler needed to get rid of those on the general staff who might oppose him, and replace them with those who would do his every bidding. He did that with every scheme possible, including charges of homosexuality, accusing wives of prostitution, and other such trumped-up charges, during what is now called the Purge of 1934.

In February, Radio Berlin, controlled by the Führer, announced a list of thirty-seven generals who had retired for 'health reasons.' Word of the 'failing health epidemic' that had riddled the ranks of Germany's generals flashed throughout the world. In the capitals of Europe, it was clear; through a series of crafty schemes and ruthless maneuvers, Adolph Hitler had gained total control of eighty million people and the now powerful armed forces.

During this period, those who understood Hitler's menace and had means to escape Germany left the country, including many of its finest minds and most talented artists. Others were unable to leave. Many, however, were more than willing to stay.

Hitler's economic policy was remarkable. He did have a lot of luck; but it was more than luck. He deliberately destroyed the trade union movement, which had restricted all free movement of labor between jobs and workplace. The effect this had in cutting unemployment was startling, as three million workers found jobs in the construction of freeways, the so-called autobahns. The German people increasingly relied on Hitler's leadership to restore national pride and prosperity and the path to war was paved.

How many knew his true goal was not just to unify all German-speaking people, or to conquer all of continental Europe and consolidate it under Nazi role, but to fight further wars that would make Germany into a global superpower? Did they know his aim was to enslave and exterminate entire peoples, especially the Jews and the Soviets? It remains incredulous to me that even today some still deny that the Holocaust really happened.

CHAPTER 5

A Hitler "What If?"

I had not known how close Hitler came to being stopped before he started the war. By 1938, many in leadership in Germany were convinced that Hitler was getting ready for a widespread war of conquest, hell bent on taking Germany on the road to eventual destruction. How right they were. As a result, a group of high-ranking officers, civilian leaders and government officials created a conspiratorial group which the Gestapo would later call Schwartze Kapelle—the Black Orchestra. It was headed by General Ludwig Beck, Chief of the German General Staff, who had directed the Army's enormous expansion during the previous three years. He was regarded by other German generals and by foreign leaders as a man of high honor and integrity.

The conspirators had managed to obtain Corporal Adolph Hitler's medical records from his service in The Great War, which seemed to indicate that Hitler had 'gone mad' as a result of being gassed. At the end of that war he was still hospitalized, temporarily blinded from the poisonous gas. Consequently, they set up a secret panel of psychiatrists to issue a report on his mental fitness.

The Black Orchestra then drew up a plan to get rid of Hitler by a coup d'état. The Führer was to be arrested in Berlin, but not killed. Rather he would be put on trial before the German people, with procedures worked out by legal experts involved with the Black Orchestra.

The keen military minds of the conspirators had created a plan in minute detail. At the proper time, General Erich Fellgiebel, chief signals officer, would cut all communications throughout Germany, thereby isolating Hitler in Berlin. At the same time, General Erwin von Wetzleben, the commander of the Berlin military district, would rush reinforcements into the capital and issue orders for them to arrest Hitler and his two top aides, General Hermann Goering and Heinrich Himmler. The latter, a former chicken farmer, was considered a rare mixture of crackpot and organizational genius. As commander of Hitler's Schutzstaffel (SS), he would have to be 'neutralized' if the conspirators' plot was to succeed.

The SS was an elite group of German Storm Troopers, which included the infamous Waffen SS. A division of the Nazi party, the SS was established in 1925, to serve as Hitler's personal guards and act as a special security force in Germany and its occupied countries during World War II. It was originally comprised of only eight men. By 1933, the year that Hitler assumed power, it had swelled to well over 200,000 members.

Hitler, Goering, Himmler, and other Nazi leaders were to be rushed southward to Bavaria by a heavily armed contingent of General von Wetzleben's soldiers, and locked up securely in the dungeon of a castle near Munich. According to the established scenario, at his trial Hitler was to be exposed as criminally insane and unfit to hold the office of Führer, because his madness had prompted him to create grandiose plans for world conquest that would forever destroy Germany as a nation.

Once the trial judges ruled that Hitler was insane, he would be safely ensconced in a mental institution, and heavily guarded around the clock. Then a civilian of prominence and respectability, not yet selected, was to form a new German government along democratic lines. But the leaders of the Black Orchestra were faced with the knotty problem of when to strike.

There were worries about doing it right away. Although German generals and admirals were almost unanimous in their contempt for the one-time army corporal, they had to deal with the fact that Hitler had the undeniable love and trust of most of the German people, and the support of the army and navy. Titans of industry were also firmly in the Führer's corner—no wonder, since business was booming. The huge military buildup was making arms manufacturers extremely wealthy men with enormous influence.

Reluctantly, the Black Orchestra decided to bide its time, waiting for Hitler to perpetrate some sort of disaster that would turn many of the German people against him. They had missed their moment. After that, several other plots were also hatched to eliminate Hitler. Needless to say, none of them succeeded. One cannot help but wonder—what if they had?

CHAPTER 6

Life on the Brink

The Depression spread hardship throughout Germany, as well as my home country, although at the time, it did not affect my family too drastically. My father was working, and so were my aunt and uncles. But there were many others it did affect. I heard about long lines and soup kitchens that barely, but ultimately, helped many people stay alive.

The war efforts of Germany began while I was a child beginning grade school. Although it was still years from reaching the Netherlands, I often heard my parents talking about war in other countries. There were early warnings of what lay ahead.

Hitler was appointed chancellor of Germany in 1933, and before the year was over, Germany withdrew from the League of Nations, which had been formed at the end of World War I. In 1936, Germany reoccupied the Rhineland in violation of the Versailles Treaty. In that same year, Germany signed an alliance with Japan—and Italy in 1937—against the Soviet Union. This was interesting in light of the earlier secret agreement between von Seeckt and Lenin after World War I.

In Austria, there was a large Nazi party. In 1938, Hitler felt free to act against Austria. He claimed he wanted to unify all German-speaking people. Dr. Arthur Seyss-Inquart, later one of the terrors of the Netherlands, was the Austrian Nazi leader, who requested so-called German "help" with Austria. When Hitler "annexed" Austria, Britain and France slapped him on the fingers, "Bad boy, bad, bad, bad boy," and that was the end of it.

With no real consequence after this test action against Austria, Hitler then felt free to start war proceedings against

Czechoslovakia, demanding liberation of German people in a Czech region, where they had voluntarily settled, just like me moving to America. In September 1938, the Treaty of Munich, in which Czechoslovakia was not even represented, conceded Hitler even more than he had demanded. The Czech president was literally forced to request a German protectorate. Even so, despite the promises in the Treaty, in March 1939 Hitler marched into Czechoslovakia. Like the Dutch later, the Czechs were not powerful enough to resist the Wehrmacht (combined military power).

I visited Prague in 2003, and noticed there was still a strong anti-German sentiment. I understood at once, It took me until 1990, when I hosted a group of German musicians, to realize that these people had not even been born at that time; they had no part in it.

Hitler had also been menacing Poland since January 1939. The Poles, however, resisted his threats. That spring, Britain and France issued a declaration guaranteeing the independence of Poland, a week before they announced they would defend Belgium, the Netherlands and Switzerland. This was a farce, but they hoped to draw in the Soviet Union for additional protection. However, Poland declined for fear that the Russians would then annex large parts of Poland as a reward for their intervention. Ironically, just a few months later that fear came true anyway, when Russia and Germany signed a non-aggression pact with secret clauses for the division of Poland between the two of them. Poland had been divided many times; but they'd always managed to spring back.

The Poles began to mobilize in July, when war loomed imminent, but did not fully deploy all of their men. They formed forty divisions, none armored. Polish tanks were old, and half of their 935 aircraft were obsolete. With the Russian-German pact of August 1939, Poland was badly outflanked on two of her borders. Still, she counted on French and British assistance to attack Germany's western border. But the French did not move on them from the west. Neither they, nor the British, were mobilized.

Now all Hitler needed was a reason to attack Poland. He would use any excuse, staged or not. In this case it was staged.

This was done by Hitler's SS near the town of Gleirich, where a so-called police aggression took place. SS troops in Polish uniforms staged a mock attack on a German radio station, leaving a drugged concentration camp inmate smeared with blood as a supposed German casualty of the attack.

* * *

On the morning of September 1, 1939, German tanks rolled across the border. Hitler issued no declaration of war. By October 6, Poland's resistance had ended, and it was defeated. About 100,000 Poles fled to neighboring countries, making their way to France and later to Britain. There, they formed the Polish armed forces in exile. They fought on until the last days of the war. My father had deep respect for the Poles. He called them heroic, fierce fighters, which they were.

On September 3, 1939, two days after Hitler attacked Poland, Britain and France declared war on Germany. However, it has been called the "Phony War," because Britain saw no military action until May 1940, after we were attacked. The French had mobilized, but the expected clash did not happen. The French army, victor over Germany in The Great War, and reputedly the world's strongest army at the time, sat with a false sense of security behind the Maginot Line, a formidable line of fortifications built in the 1930s from the Swiss to the Belgian borders. They were unwilling to stick out their necks at that time.

Every summer, we left the city and went to the country during our six weeks of school vacation, from mid-July until the end of August. My father never had six weeks of vacation, and so had to commute from wherever we rented a cottage or part of a house, in Baarn, Bussem, or Huizen. He rode his bicycle to Amsterdam in the morning and back home after work every night. Baarn was the farthest—35 kilometers, more than 20 miles—each way. What dedication to his family he demonstrated during those days.

In the summer of 1939, while we were on vacation away from the city, the Netherlands mobilized its men. I recall an endless line of men having to report. The wait for them apparently was very long, for a lot of them had sprawled out in the grass, on the side of the road. My mother and my aunt, both young women, went down to them with water and sandwiches which they provided free of charge, not to all, of course, because there were too many, but to those waiting to report at the end of the street near to where we were staying.

French commanders considered an attack against northeastern France most unlikely, choosing to ignore the gap reaching from the end of the Maginot Line to the English Channel. They also considered the hilly, forested Ardennes area between France and Belgium to be too difficult to penetrate, an unlikely site for a major German attack. This left the Liege area of Belgium, which led to the flatlands of Flanders and then to France's northern frontier, as the main path likely open to the Germans. And indeed that was the initial plan of the Germans.

The French and British leaders, in a kind of war-weary lethargy, decided it would be good enough to move into Belgium once the Germans attacked. They assumed they could buy time by delaying action by the Belgian army, taking advantage of the barrier of the Ardennes and the Meuse River, the large forts at Liege, the deep cut of the Albert Canal north of that city, and Fort Eben-Emael near the Dutch-Belgian border, said to be the strongest single fortress in the world.

France and Britain waited for months, as the German attack was delayed several times due to bad weather. Further complicating things was that during those eight months, although expecting an invasion of the Lowlands (The Netherlands, Belgium, and Luxembourg), the Allies failed to consult and coordinate with the Belgians and Dutch. This was fine with the Lowlands, which had remained neutral during World War I, and had carefully attempted to do so at this time as well. All were assured of Germany's peaceful intent. The main strategy was neutrality. For the Dutch, the war remained in the background, and apparently for its neighboring Allies also.

In April of 1940, German forces invaded Denmark and Norway, wanting to safeguard supply routes of Swedish ore, and to establish a Norwegian base from which to break the British naval blockade on Germany. Denmark surrendered immediately, but the Norwegians kept fighting until they lost French support in June.

These invasions led France and Britain to accept the imminent and growing threat of the Nazis, but by then it was too late. Just one month later—May of 1940—Hitler turned his attention to the Low Countries. We were Germany's neighbor to the northwest, and he feared the Allies would attack Germany through the Netherlands. Germany also desperately needed Dutch airfields to supply its advancing forces; so the attack began.

The combined French, Dutch, Belgian and British forces available were four million men, compared to two million Germans. In tanks and aircraft, the opposing forces were relatively equal. Yet Hitler prevailed through strategy—and the absence of our Allies—until it was too late. Holland alone was no match for Germany.

In May of 1940, the Leibstandarte—Bodyguard Regiment—overcame Dutch border guards. Thus, the Germans advanced into Holland, heading toward Rotterdam. After the surrender of Rotterdam, they moved on to The Hague, where they captured over 3,500 Dutch prisoners of war.

CHAPTER 7

War Comes to the Lowlands

The morning of May 10, 1940, I woke up to the sound of the radio. Something unusual was happening. Paratroopers had landed at Schiphol, our largest airport. We did not have to go to school. For a ten year old, this was wonderful of course. My sister and I went outside to jump rope.

Being a city kid, and living on the top floor of our building, we never had much contact with neighbors. Perhaps they would have been friendlier, but you just did not see each other that much, typical for city people. But that day in Amsterdam, people were milling about everywhere. I never saw so many people outside, including the butcher and his employees, and the bookstore owner and his helpers.

The second day was no longer much fun. Even as kids we knew something was really wrong. Our Queen issued a protest statement. How naïve to think a man like Hitler would react to a protest statement! But meanwhile the government was preparing to flee, unlike King Leopold from Belgium, who refused to leave his people. How wise this decision was no one really knows; but he stayed.

The Netherlands had stayed neutral from World War I onward, thinking to keep our small country safe that way. Over the years, our pacifist leaders let our defenses fall to a deplorable state. By the time we realized Hitler would not leave us in peace, and laws were passed to improve our defenses, there was not enough time to modernize our old-fashioned army. When the Germans invaded, we had reached only forty percent of our goals. Half of our artillery dated back to 1880. Our only real tank was from World War I, although we did have twenty-eight light armored cars that were of some use in defending the airfields from paratroopers. We had one hundred twenty planes, half of them dual-wings intended for reconnaissance, and only nine bombers.

The Dutch Army was under the command of General Henri Gerard Winkelman. Before mobilization we had only 90,000 troops; after mobilization, we had 280,000. By comparison, our southern neighbor, Belgium, had 650,000. More importantly, we were pitted against an enemy of 460,000 Germans, well trained and equipped with modern gear.

Long before this, it was realized we could not defend the whole country against a German invasion, but instead would focus on defending the western part, which contained the large city of Amsterdam; the Hague, government seat and home of the royal family; and Rotterdam, then—and still today—the largest port in the world.

Holland with its many water ways and soggy land had formed a defense line by flooding a large part of the country, during wars in the Middle Ages and beyond. During World War II, the defense strategy was called Fortress Holland. It involved defense works among the many rivers and canals of the area, most dating back to the Middle Ages; many are still there today. The strategy that had existed for hundreds of years was that when an attack was imminent, we would slowly pull back behind these defense lines. The deserted terrain would then be flooded.

The idea was to delay the advance of enemy troops long enough for our Allies to come to our rescue. It was ruled out because our largest cities were in this area, and would be impossible to evacuate. So due to the fact that there were now twelve million people occupying our very soil, along with growth of the large cities, this proved to be impossible as a line of defense during World War II.

Their invasion was a daring, revolutionary strike from the air. All of Germany's 30,000 landing forces, and the major part of its air force, were put into action in the Netherlands. Never before had so many paratroopers landed in such a short time on enemy territory. I remember the sky being full of parachutes. They had pierced the final Dutch defense line. French advance guards arrived on May 11, attempting to reinforce and hold the line with Dutch forces; but by May 13, they were forced to retreat.

A German airborne landing at The Hague intended to capture the Dutch royal family but failed. On May 13, our queen, as well as the cabinet, escaped to England. Since it was thought to be safer, our princess with her family left for Ottawa, Canada. How Queen Wilhelmina must have missed seeing her granddaughters grow up during the years she could not see them. But not only did the royal family and the cabinet escape, but our submarines and their crews did as well, and continued to fight on with the Allies from an Australian base.

Because of the large number of Dutch submarines active in the waters near Japan, the Dutch were named the Fourth Ally, along with the Australians, Americans, and New Zealanders. Many of our pilots also escaped, and with airplanes given to us by the United States they formed two squadrons, and were successful in defending Australia from the Japanese. They participated in the liberation of the Dutch East Indies.

After the attacks on the Low Countries, the 'Phony War' became a real one. On May 13, Winston Churchill became the new head of the wartime coalition government, and returned as first lord of the admiralty. The British Expeditionary Force stationed 250,000 troops alongside the French at the north end of the Maginot Line, all expecting Germany to invade France from the east.

But ultimately the Allied forces ended up with their backs to the English Channel, trapped between two German Armies in northern France. German Army Group A had burst through the Ardennes region, supposedly impenetrable, and advanced rapidly to the west, then turned north to the Channel. Army Group B invaded to the east and subdued the Netherlands, advancing westward through Belgium. With no escape route by land, Allied evacuation by sea was the only option. But the beach waters were too shallow for military ships; so the British designed Operation Dynamo.

On the morning of May 14, the Germans warned that if resistance continued, the port of Rotterdam would be destroyed from the air. The city surrendered, but bombers already en route were not called back. Two hours before the ultimatum was to expire, the Luftwaffe leveled Rotterdam, inflicting enormous damage in the heart of the city; the only thing left standing was a church tower. It cost an incalculable number of civilian casualties and resulted in widespread homelessness.

Published estimates indicated eight hundred civilians were killed and one-third of the city destroyed, but this seems small compared to the reports of devastation. I remember my aunt, who had a lot of family in Rotterdam, saying her family told her body parts were hanging in the trees. I am grateful never to have seen any of that; I imagine it would have been extremely difficult to overcome.

There were reports of locations where the Dutch Army offered strong resistance. There had been fierce fighting around a large bridge in Rotterdam, which was held by ten Marines for several days. All ten eventually died. Fighting was also fierce around the Grebbeberg, where one of my cousins was trying to hold up a German tank with a rifle from 1914. More up-to-date weapons had been ordered but had not arrived. The Afsluitdijk (closing dyke) was another one of the places. It was hopeless of course, but they did what they could.

The next cities in the ultimatum were Utrecht, which is in the middle of the country, followed by Amsterdam. It was surrender 'or else.' With the nation's defenses decimated, and no hope of Allied aid from anywhere, General Winkelman surrendered late on May 14. Our war lasted just five days. Considering how poorly our Dutch army was equipped, one might say it's a wonder it lasted that long. The fighting did continue in the province of Zeeland, however, until after the bombardment of Middelburg on May 17.

When bombs started falling, my parents realized we needed to have something to identify each of us; at first this was a circular piece of bone, tied by a piece of rope, which we wore around our necks. It was made of bone so that in the event of burning, we would still be identifiable by these tags. Later, they had new ones made of metal with our names engraved into them. Still, these tags hung around our necks with simple pieces of rope. This would not have survived any fire, of course, but the hope was that if any of us perished, the ID tag, which we referred to as 'dog tags,' similar to what the military used for soldiers, would be found at least near our remains.

In our case, our full names were way too long to put on the engraved metal dog tags. As such, we had to resort to using our first initials with our full last name, along with our birth dates. Fortunately, none of my family ever needed identification by 'dog tag.' Miraculously, we all managed to survive this horrific war.

One sad measure of how hard we fought was the loss of life. Norway and Denmark had been defeated with only minor losses. My fellow countrymen were stunned that our small nation lost 2,600 civilians and 2,300 soldiers, in addition to 7,000 wounded. Still, the Germans lost 45,000 people in the combined three countries of the Lowlands. After the air invasion of Holland, which decimated their airborne troops and destroyed 328 of their 1,024 aircraft, the Germans never again would carry out such a large scale air landing operation. They learned that lesson at our expense; but how great that we managed to down that many of their planes.

We lived on a major thoroughfare. If there were dignitaries coming through, we always watched by leaning out of the windows, three stories up. We had to be careful not to lean too far for fear of falling out of the window. From these windows, we saw the occupying hoards coming through on May 16. There were rows upon rows of proudly marching soldiers, trying to impress us with their parade steps. Oh, how I remember the sound of German troops marching down our street, the proud conquerors letting us know that they were mighty, that we were in their power, and that they were out to win the war.

Within days of my own country being invaded, Hitler's massed troops, spearheaded by dive bombers and paratroopers poured into Belgium with an armored assault the likes of which had never been seen before. Three columns of tanks roared in, slicing Allied forces in half, trapping the British and French divisions.

On May 24, a call went out to civilian owners of vessels. They used anything that would float—pleasure boats, steamers, launches, fishing boats, and barges. The evacuation began May 26, and by June 4, some 900 boats had rescued 338,000 troops, including 140,000 of the Free French Army under Charles de Gaulle. They left behind 2,300 pieces of artillery, 82,000 vehicles, 90,000 rifles, 8,000 automatic (sten) machine guns, 400 anti-tank rifles and 7,000 tons of ammunition. But the men had been saved.

The German task force had been practicing on replica targets during the previous winter. Belgium's Fort Eben-Emael, mentioned earlier, was a steel and concrete fort, thought to be impregnable. It was dug deep into the soil, had gun turrets, and was manned by over 1,200 warriors. The Germans landed on the fort by gliders. Specially made explosives knocked out the gun turrets, spreading flames everywhere, as did the flame throwers, blinding the defenders. Panzer units (short for Panzerkampfwagen, the German word for 'tank') and dive bombers finished the job. The Belgians capitulated on May 28.

On June 5, 1940, Dunkirk (Dunkerque) fell to the Germans. They continued their push south and west through France, entering Paris on June 14. On June 15, over 200,000 British troops still in France began evacuating from French ports that remained in Allied hands. On June 17, Pétain became the French premier, and negotiated an armistice signed on June 22 which formally took France out of the war and into German occupation. My parents were stunned. They had figured a large country like France—and winner of World War I—would halt the German war machine.

CHAPTER 8

Early Occupation and Resistance

After the brief Dutch war came the German occupation and resistance sprang up almost immediately. On May 18, just three days after the capitulation, the Geuzen Acte letters started. The Geuzen were the Dutch heroes who fought against Spanish tyranny and the Inquisition in the Netherlands during the 80-Year War of the 1500s. The process involved a resister delivering two handwritten letters to two people he or she trusted, asking the receivers of the letters to do the same, giving letters to people they could trust. This was like a chain letter, if you will, with whatever news one could glean. It was a very small start; the news was gathered by people who had ham radios, and for the time being all we would hear was what the enemy wanted us to hear. It was also the start of the Dutch underground. The Dutch underground was formed by men and women without military training, but with the strong desire to help conquer the enemy. Casualties therefore were very high.

Not all Dutch were resisters. There was in the Netherlands—as in Germany—a party, the National Socialist Beweging (NSB), which means national socialist movement. It was a home grown Nazi Party. It was the only allowed political party in the Netherlands during the occupation, after 1941. These people loved Hitler and all he stood for. People were poor just after The Great Depression, and clung to all who promised to improve their lot. The NSB did that. They were Nazi sympathizers, mostly younger families, but not all. They were a minority— only three percent of the adult male population in 1941, when Germany still seemed to be winning the war. But they were a minority to be feared. They wore black uniforms, like Hitler's SS, the ruthless elite guards. Their leader was a middle-aged engineer by the name of Anton Mussert. The man had married his aunt who was eighteen years older than he was. You should have heard all of the jokes that were made about that,

Our country's lack of woods, coupled with the fact that the population was so dense, made it very difficult to do anything illicit. Ads started to appear in the newspaper with hidden meanings and messages, a tricky way to show resistance. I have a photo book showing a real ad from that time, of a pastry shop selling cookies named for the queen: "Our Wilhelmina cookies are still in great demand. Does that mean anything to you? Try them." At the bottom of the ad it said, "Next week you'll find New Sorts of Butter cookies," and then gave the name of the store. The bold initials at the start of the words were a subtle jibe at the NSB. Putting it at the bottom of the ad meant they were the lowest. This was a dangerous sort of thing to publish; but we got the message, and we loved those little digs.

Dr. Arthur Seyss-Inquart, who had been head of Austria's Nazi party, became the Netherlands' head of government; this was very bad for us. He was ruthless. By German directive, we had to put black blinds in front of our windows. My mother had beautiful burgundy velour drapes which she hung over the black ones, so the inside of our home still looked lovely. They would shoot at the window if any light was shining out. This was to prevent the Allied airplanes from seeing where they were, and using the city lights as a beacon. Some got lost on occasion, but most reached their destination anyway.

Princess Juliana's husband, Prince Bernhard, was known to always wear a white carnation in the lapel of his suit coats. His birthday was June 29. In 1940, thousands who ordinarily could have not cared less about his birthday appeared wearing white carnations. This was the first massive demonstration against the oppressor.

It was customary that at the birthday of one of the royal family, a register was put out for people to sign, and then it would be forwarded to the particular celebrant. That year, there were so many signing the register that extra pages had to be brought in. German planes circled overhead the whole day. The mayor of The Hague was fired the next day. With the prince either in Canada or England, forwarding the signed register was impossible. But the message was clear. The Netherlanders were beginning to rise up.

In the summer of 1940, the Germans had several films made to encourage fraternization. Initially the German policy in the Netherlands was that the Dutch nation was to be dissolved and become part of a Germanic or Aryan Nation of Lords. The most important German officials, including the SS, Seyss-Inquart and Hitler himself, regarded the Dutch non-Jews as part of the Aryan Herrenvolk. NO, NO, NO, we are not your brethren! They thought they could just annex us, like they had done to Austria.

The Battle of Britain began July 10, 1940. The Luftwaffe attacked British ports, then RAF airfields, and later came the Blitz of London. Oh those poor Brits! Night after night we could hear the drone of the German planes heading for London. The British RAF defended the skies, and by October 31, the raids had ceased. The Germans abandoned their plans to invade Britain; one would wonder why, had they invaded, the outcome of the war could have been so different. Thank God, they did not!

We felt so bad for the British, but later this was a sound we relished when the Allied forces would go overhead to bomb Germany. For those poor people in London, how unnerving this must have been, night after night, remembering how frightened my mother was when there was a bombing raid. At the time, I was too young to truly be scared; if I think about it now I am sure I would be scared, just like my mother.

In September, Italy and Japan signed a pact to officially become Hitler's allies. The Netherlands now had the WA volunteer militia, a part of the NSB, like the SA militia earlier in Germany. In the winter of 1940-41, groups of them would march to downtown Amsterdam and start fights. They were the lowest of the low, just young men looking for any reason to get violent.

CHAPTER 9

Jews Targeted

In 1939, there were some 140,000 Jews living in the Netherlands, among them some 25,000 German-Jewish refugees who had fled Germany in the 1930s. In 1941, the majority of Dutch Jews were living in Amsterdam, which today is still considered the center of Jewish life in the Netherlands. The Dutch underground hid a large number of Jews during the war, but in 1945, only about 35,000 were still alive. Some seventy-five percent of the Dutch Jewish population perished, one of the highest percentages of all Nazi-occupied countries, despite the fact that Dutch Jews seemed to be more tolerated by and integrated into the Dutch population than, for example, the Jews in Poland.

The Dutch identity card was changed to indicate either B1 or B2. As non-Jews, we were officially B1. The B2 meant bastard and was issued only to Jews. It could not have been more hurtful. We all had identity cards, even the children. I saved mine, as well as my 'dog tags' and have them to this day.

The terrorizing of Jews had started. Every establishment now had to post a sign: "voor Joden verboden"—"Jews Not Allowed." The owner of a particular café had refused to do this, and the WA, a Dutch division of the Waffen SS, destroyed the man's business establishment. Jews were exiled from normal Dutch society. Jews in professions such as dentists, doctors, and lawyers were forbidden to have any other patients or clients except Jews. We had found another doctor when we moved; for them the indignities occurred daily. My girlfriend Edith now had to wear the Star of David sewn on her clothes. In Belgium the

43

entire population, even non-Jews, wore the Star of David as a sign of solidarity. How courageous!

I remember an ice cream salon about ten minutes from our house. It was owned by two Jewish gentlemen who had escaped Berlin, where they had owned an identical business. They were good businessmen, had fancy names for their ice creams, as well as waitresses in cute outfits. And if my memory serves me right, it was great ice cream. The salon had only been open a couple of years, but their business was going strong. However, there was another ice cream parlor in the same street on the opposite side which seemingly was not doing well. The store's owner decided to get rid of the competition—the two Jewish guys. What better way to do this than asking for help from a family member who was a member of the WA? In they went with a group and destroyed everything they possibly could; all the glass, including the mirrors throughout the entire store, was smashed. There you have it; just another way to get rid of the competition. The two men who had so bravely fled Berlin were detained and never seen again, to my knowledge.

Our neighbor next door, above the grocery store on the second floor, was a ballerina; her husband was a violinist. She was a Gentile; he a Jew. She managed to hide him for four years in the apartment. No one noticed he was there, even though we had Nazi sympathizers across the street above the bakery. This is almost unbelievable. For four years he could never even be near a window.

Because of the cruel handling of our Jewish neighbors and the first deportation of a small group of Jews to concentration camp Mauthausen, our nation went on strike. The strike of February 25 and 26, 1941, was the first massive protest in occupied Holland. No public transportation. No mail. Stores were closed. My father stayed home from work. The tension in town was palpable. Reliving it in thought, I break out in goose bumps. The strike was unique in the history of Nazi occupied Europe.

A large number of police—and 'green police,' which were also part of the NSB—were on patrol near the palace in Amsterdam. Just one of several palaces owned by the royal family, the police swept the area every five minutes or so. People were shot; those who were wounded and survived were transported to the nearest hospital.

After the two-day strike, some streetcars were running again. They were few and far between and nearly empty. The drivers were forced to work. However, a passenger who wanted to board was told he would be beaten if he did so. A choir of conductors, waiting near the Haarlemmermeer station, reportedly warned people not to board by yelling out: "Good Dutch people don't ride the tram. Take your bicycle."

The city of Amsterdam was divided in North, South, East and West, each with its own set of tram tracks, a tram shelter, and last but not least the tram that transported people to and from work, and where ever else they needed to go. The trams were, and still are, numbered. In the neighborhood where I was living we took Tram Number 4. So indeed it was a great inconvenience when no trams were running, as happened toward the end of the war.

The strike sent a message, but proved to be a futile protest. And to think that Seyss-Inquart thought he could win us over; the Germans retaliated, of course. The three men from Amsterdam who were the leaders of the strike were executed on March 18, 1941, along with fifteen from one of the earliest resistance groups. Another three, because they were still in their late teens, were sentenced to life in prison. They were, of course, set free after the end of the war; that is, if they survived the four years of unimaginable imprisonment.

No more delusions by German leadership that the Dutch were going to be their partners in an Aryan nation. No more efforts to win us over to the Nazi cause. We were now treated strictly as enemies.

Amsterdam was fined fifteen million gulden because of the strike. That was the equivalent of fifteen million US dollars. This was to be recovered from people making more than 10,000 gulden a year, which did not include us. As a people, we were trampled and furious. This had been tried before, but never met with success. The feeling of hatred was mounting. The overall feeling was, 'Hitler, you cannot win the Dutch; others have tried before you and failed.'

Why did the protest originate in Amsterdam? We had almost 100,000 Jewish neighbors. We were the only city in which a part could be closed off by barbed wire, which was promptly done. Although not a ghetto, it was under guard by German soldiers and the WA militia. This was only the start of the manic manhunt.

In April of 1941, the Nazis forced on the Jewish community a Judenrat (Jewish Council), ostensibly to organize the identification and deportation of Jews more efficiently. Twenty prominent Jews were appointed to the council, which was chaired by Professor David Cohen and Abraham Asscher. Its first meeting was held at the Asscher Diamond Factory. They saw their role as offering protection against Nazi anti-Semitism, best achieved by complying with Nazi orders. They put out the word that the Jews would be safe, as long as they all came to register themselves. The vast majority did so, rather than jeopardize the Jewish community as uncooperative. On June 23, 1943, they had to report for so called resettlement. I still remember lots of Jewish people waiting at two places in Amsterdam. The Daniel Willink Plein (Square), which was named Victorie Plein after the war, was the closest to us; I did not observe the other. It is so unbelievable that this happened. What a sad sight seeing the poor souls standing there with their suitcases, and the few belongings they thought they would need. Some had their jewelry sewn in the hem of their overcoats, thinking to keep it safe that way. They were herded in cattle cars, without any sanitation, water or food. Just the picture of that makes me cringe. Of course, we now know that none of their belongings survived, nor did most of the deportees.

On the third floor, three houses from us, lived the Pronts. They had two boys. Their father was a Jewish man, their mother a Gentile. I had a mad secret crush on David, the oldest boy, who was a year older than I was. Suddenly, both boys disappeared, only to turn up again after the war. We knew they had gone into hiding somewhere, but we did not dare ask. It was better not to know so their secret could not be given away.

By the time council members realized that deportation did not mean sending the fittest to German labor camps, but routing all registrants to death camps, they had already given the Germans what they wanted—a comprehensive registry of Jews. In September of 1943, council members themselves were deported to Westerbork, a transit camp that routed on to non-Dutch concentration camps. Of the council members, only Cohen and Asscher were not sent on to the death camps, presumably in thanks for "services rendered." After the war, they were tried for collaborating with the enemy.

With focus on promoting fear, death, and destruction, the SS were directly responsible for establishing the concentration camps. They were in direct pursuit of locating and murdering millions of Jews, along with millions of other innocent people throughout Europe.

As the registration process led to summons and deportations, Jews went into hiding. Food was rationed. The key means of wartime consumption was rationing. Each person received a coupon booklet on a monthly basis. In order to procure anything from food to clothing, the appropriate ration coupon would need to be produced. Not allowed to be used as cash, the ration coupons were a form of additional controlled currency.

This now had entered each individual household as we had to do with much less. Starting just after the occupation, our stores were being plundered already, but even that got worse when time went on. It also entered into national politics. By mid 1942, virtually all goods had to be obtained through ration coupons. There were some unspecified coupons for certain items, such as sweets, cigarettes, and canned goods. The system required us to register with local shops. In our case this was relatively convenient. The butcher was downstairs on the ground floor of the building in which we lived. The grocer was next door to the butcher. The pastry shop was two houses down. The green grocer was two houses around the corner.

Even during wartime, the Dutch made fine pastries a priority, albeit a much scarcer, and hence more valuable, treat. We frequented the pastry shop next to the bookstore. Due to rations, we had to bring our own sugar and butter to the shop. The pastry shop would not otherwise have had enough of either ingredient to make the treats their patrons treasured so much.

The pastry shop across the street was owned by two middle-aged Jewish ladies who shared a house. In their shop were Jewish sweets, such as gember bolus and rum babas. A popular shop, they were frequented by Jews seeking traditional Jewish sweets, breads, and other Jewish foods. One night, both women were hauled out of their home and taken to a concentration camp. Neither one returned. The same fate had befallen them as six millions other Jews.

While ration coupons did not include the procurement of books, they did allow for one pair of shoes per person per year, as well as a limited amount of clothing. Again, this was convenient for us, for Roeg's Dry Goods store was simply across the street. For my family, we shopped regularly at each of these shops, so registering at each was not a problem.

The stores were allotted goods in accordance to the number of registered individuals. Each person, even small children, had their own ration coupon booklet. When an item was procured, the shop server would stamp our booklets to show we had 'cashed in' a coupon for that month. Whoever sheltered Jewish people needed extra ration coupons. With the help of good Dutch civil servants, this was still possible. When the number of people that went underground became too large, resistance groups broke into the government offices where ration coupons were kept.

The communist CPN, to which my uncle belonged, organized resistance from the start of the war. There were a lot of small groups had absolutely no link with each other. These groups produced forged ration cards, and counterfeit money, sabotaged phone lines and railways, prepared maps, collected intelligence, and distributed food and goods. My father did his part with the food and goods distribution.

My mother's oldest sister lived in the neighborhood, at house number thirteen in the Cornelis Springer Straat (Street) on the first floor. Numbers thirteen and eleven shared a common stairway, with a large landing. During one of my visits, I had met Edith, who was approximately six months older than I was. From then on, my visits always included playing with Edith; I was no longer bored having to sit with the adults. They had several Jewish neighbors, including a family of four at number thirteen, one floor below at street level, as well as my friend Edith and her family in number eleven, also on the first floor.

In 1942, the family who lived below my aunt and uncle somehow had gotten wind of a pending raid, and decided they would have to flee; their only crime was being born Jewish. My aunt, always a bit naïve, thought my mom could fix anything. So she sent the Jewish family to our house. We had no extra beds or rooms, and they slept in chairs for the couple of nights they stayed with us. In this case my mother couldn't 'fix' it for long, but we accepted the danger, and, I hope, helped them by doing so. Never did we hear from those people after the war; we can only hope they survived.

The summer camp for children, next door to where we vacationed in Huizen, had now been requisitioned by the Germans. The field, where the year before the farmer was still harvesting his grain, was now being used as training ground for the militia, as well as the Waffen SS. They loved to march singing their songs. My sister and I learned to sing their songs, which was all we had heard for six weeks. Back at home, we would be washing dishes and singing their songs, accompanying ourselves by taking wooden spoons and banging on my mother's pans, to accompany our beautiful music—at least we thought so.

Traitors were everywhere. No one knew whom to trust. Informants would tell the authorities where Jewish people were hiding for payment of only 7.50 gulden per person, about $8. How could anyone sell another human being, for any amount of money? This thought never occurred to me when my fourth grade 'boyfriend' sold me to his friend for a decent profit. How prophetic that moment would become.

It also meant that families who had been willing to shelter the Jews were either shot to death or sent to a concentration camp, where most would die anyway. One-third of the people who hid Jews did not survive the war. My friend Edith Pachter's father was a small man who worked as a presser for a drycleaners about a ten-minute walk from their home. The Pachters had five children; Edith was the middle child. There were two older girls, the eldest of which was an extremely pretty young woman who was married to a Gentile. The next elder sister was about age 16, and Edith was 13. I don't remember much about the younger two.

Between Christmas 1942 and the beginning of January 1943, the girls in my class and I went to a youth hostel in the country. I wrote and directed a short play which was great fun. Earlier, my sister and I were in a children's operetta—what we call musical theater today—along with my friend Edith, who portrayed a boy, since they were always in short supply. Little did we know that would be the last fun thing she did.

When I came back from the country, I learned that Edith and the rest of her family still living at home had been deported to Auschwitz. Not one of them ever returned. Her elder sister, Esther, who had married the Gentile, was the only one to have survived. However, she was forced to have a tubal ligation to prevent her from having children. It was hard on me, losing my friend, Edith. I cannot possibly imagine what Esther must have felt, having lost her entire family, and never being able to have children of her own.

On a winter evening, in January of 1943, a razzia (raid) took place across the street. This was only a few weeks after Edith and her family had been deported, further evidence of the manic manhunt. As was customary, it went hand in hand with a lot of shouting. It happened during the evening that I saw both elderly neighbors, the Roegs, the store owners who were in their seventies, being hauled out of their house, clubbed with rifle butts, and shoved into a truck.

Earlier, their son Johnny had escaped to England, where he enlisted in the Dutch armed forces. He came back in 1945 at the war's end, only to learn that his parents had been taken away by force and never returned. He moved back into the family home, married, and had a son named Nicky. He then adopted a child of a family member whose parents had perished, but had managed to find a family to shelter their son, also named Nicky (Nicolas). Therefore, after the war, we had small Nicky and big Nicky both across the street from us.

On nights when we were having dinner, we had one of many police (in this case Gestapo) visits. When they entered our living room, the first thing they always blurted out was, "Sind Sie Juden?" meaning "Are you Jews?" We could honestly deny that, but I had to think, if one was a Jew, could one have truly denied it? All of this again, thanks to the informants who lived across the street and spied on all of us.

CHAPTER 10

More on the Early War

Germany fed itself from its own agricultural output as well as food requisitioned from occupied lands, including the Netherlands. Although not hungry, we had to eat foods different from what we were used to. But we had not yet experienced real hunger. I liked to drink tea, but it was then made from some sort of a tablet and tasted horrible. Sugar was soon also in short supply. To this day I cannot tolerate the taste of saccharine or any other kind of artificial sweetener.

For four years, during the occupation, my parents still took us on vacation to the country in summer. For a brief period of time in 1940 or 1941, due to concerns about the dangers of the city, my sister and I went to school in the country, at Baarn. At this time my father commuted by bike as he had during our vacations. My mother was right about finding the city too dangerous, because again bombs had missed their target, and some fell in the Carillon Street, which was about a five-minute walk from our home. Too close for comfort, she thought.

My parents were city dwellers; I think my mother got bored with country life fast. There was not enough room for everyday life in the partial-villa we rented. And it was not practical for my father to commute by bicycle in the winter months in Holland with its abundant rain and wind.

In 1943, both of my parents were hospitalized. My mother was in one hospital, having a severe bout of sciatica, and was put into traction. My father, in a different hospital, was suffering from seizures. Being the eldest, and with no parents at home, it was my responsibility to provide for my brothers and sister.

It was at this time that I first learned to cook. I remember asking the lady that lived on the second floor how to cook green beans. This was my one and only cooking lesson from her. Earlier, I had learned to make mashed potatoes in school.

I got so proficient at cooking that my brother, Johnny, said, "Wat Hans maakt, smaakt," which translates into "What Hans makes, tastes good." And from this need to provide for my siblings, in order that we survive, began a lifelong love of cooking.

* * *

The Netherlands has the North Sea and Britain to its west and Germany to its east. The Germans were fighting over us, not as a people, but literally above our heads. Back in the city, because of the ever-increasing number of dogfights above the city, and the fact that both top floors next to and across from us were riddled with bullet holes, my mother thought it wise to hang comforters in front of the glass doors, in hopes that we could be spared injury, at least from flying glass.

We had grown used to the almost daily drumming of the Allied bombers, and the thump-thump of the German anti-aircraft guns. We recognized the sounds, and knew the locations somewhat. One was on the east side of town by the cemetery, and sounded like a dog yelping. I hated the sight of the search lights; I could see the airplanes caught in the search light, like a fly in a spider's web. In 1941, I was eleven years old. I saw an airplane shot down, spinning as they do, and a man baling out in a parachute. He was so close I could see his face. He was helpless. They'd shot him. The bastards! It is something that still brings me to tears, and that I will never forget. As I started to write this down, I found myself sobbing after all those years. What a wonderful purging experience this recount of my youth has been; I had kept it bottled up all those years.

Then there was the wailing of the air raid sirens. Sirens and I still do not agree. They built an air raid shelter across from my school. It looked like a hill, all green with grass. Once there was an air raid during school and they herded us all in there. It smelled really bad; I am pretty sure that men had used it as a toilet facility. I question if it would have kept us alive in case of a direct hit. Fortunately, we never had to find out.

In early 1941, Hitler's forces pushed their armies into Yugoslavia, Macedonia, Serbia, Croatia, Greece and Crete, briefly held and defended by the Brits and New Zealanders. The German parachutists suffered enormous losses. In one village they were attacked by women and children using any weapon they could find, even pitchforks. A great many Germans were wounded. Yet when German reinforcements arrived, again Adolph Hitler had the upper hand.

The Germans crowed about their winning, and for a while it looked like it would never go our way. They seemed unbeatable. They loved to print and put out posters and placards, placing them on kiosks, bare walls, literally everywhere they could find space. We walked a long way to school and saw a lot on the way. One poster said, "Germany is winning on all fronts." Overnight someone painted on that poster, "April Fool."

Resistance members who were pasting posters during the night were shot on the spot if they were caught, or if they were "lucky" sent to a concentration camp. Still they managed to paint or paste anti-German messages, and gave us warnings and news that wouldn't otherwise reach us. They encouraged, "Don't enlist in the German Army." They said, "Resist, resist, resist and sabotage." The message was clear even to us kids. There were actually men that did enlist in the German Army. I learned that there were between 20,000 and 25,000 volunteers. A lot of them served in the Waffen SS, of which the most notable formation was the Fourth SS Volunteer Panzer Grenadier Brigade Nederland, which saw action on the Eastern front, and the Landstorm Nederland, which harassed us in both Belgium and The Netherlands.

Due to censorship, the radio and newspapers were only allowed to deliver the news approved by the Germans, which obviously only reported the positive results of the German war effort. A large newspaper in the southern part of Netherlands was closed, I assume, for trying to report things more honestly.

There were Dutch-speaking broadcasts from London, on Radio Oranje (Radio Orange). These provided the real news to the illegal newspapers. Of course, it was with great difficulty that the first radio contact with England was made. Those who got caught doing it were executed for forbidden sender contact.

Though the first illegal newsletters were handwritten or typed, they had grown to a number of regularly appearing papers. They called for sabotage and resistance. This caused much grief to the oppressors, who did everything in their power to get the journalistic "guilty parties." Of course, we did not think they were guilty at all, but rather very courageous.

While at school, a teacher asked me if I would deliver underground newspapers to two families in my neighborhood. These were printed whenever there was enough news to be spread around to the Dutch. I agreed and carried them between my school books. My parents never knew; they never would have given me permission to do this. But I was fourteen years old and, as all children at that age think they are, invincible. I had no fear at that time, so when my teacher got newspapers from her source, she would give me the two copies to deliver. I would go to the two houses where she wanted me to bring them, ring the doorbell, climb the stairs, and hand deliver the paper to whoever opened the door. It was not like the regular newspapers; we did get regular newspapers too, but they only contained the news the Germans wanted us to see. There was no cost for the paper; it was totally clandestine. Someone actually asked me this upon my telling them about the paper.

Someone shot a German officer. Because of that, ten men were rounded up and shot. My Uncle Henk was in the resistance, as well as his sister and her husband. They were betrayed and Henk was sent to Buchenwald, a concentration camp in eastern Germany. They were accused of being communist Jew lovers, among other things. I will tell his story later. It was around this time that the CPN became better organized.

And so it continued. Weekly one of the many sympathizers was shot, and then the resisters faced reprisal. Toward the end of the war it was not even targeted at partisans after the attacks, killings became random acts. Our partisans—resisters—had many false papers now, which gave them the opportunity to play every part necessary to do their dangerous work: Gestapo policemen, nurses, and so on. Armed with that, they plotted a complete drawing of the defenses the enemy had built along our coastline and forwarded it to England, not knowing where the invasion would take place.

But spying went both ways. Before the war, there were many German maidens working in the Netherlands, usually as domestic help. My father's younger brother, who owned a bicycle repair shop, married one of them. Unfortunately, many of them also served as spies, and had drawn diagrams and mapped out all of our fortifications and other important resources and provided these to the Germans.

My father came home with a lot of stuff, bought or traded for us on the black market. Across from us, on the third floor, lived a family who were members of the NSB. This neighbor tipped off the police, who came to search and managed to find nothing. I think they must have been "good" policemen, who needed to follow up on the tip but weren't about to find a reason to turn us in. We were fortunate that time, since many in the police force had been replaced by Nazi sympathizers.

We went to a Christian school. Every morning we had a half hour of Bible reading and prayer, which was done by none other than our principal. His son was in the resistance, which of course, we did not know until the young man was executed. His father prayed openly in class for the Lord to help us to defeat the enemy, even though we had several boys in class belonging to the Hitler Youth. Our principal took an enormous risk, but felt so strongly about the issue, he just could not keep his mouth shut.

Among the traitorous informants, the most notorious was a man out of Rotterdam named van der Waals, whose betrayals caused the death of several hundred people, men and women. He was paid well for this, the Judas. In 1943, an announcement appeared in the papers that he was gravely wounded in an assault and died on the way to the hospital. This was an intentional deception from the enemy to make the Resistance think the man was dead. But he was alive and well. So awful were his crimes, that he was executed by the Dutch Government in 1946, something very unusual in the Netherlands.

CHAPTER 11

The War Expands

Despite the 1939 non-aggression pact, on June 22, 1941, Hitler invaded Russia. The news that Hitler attacked Russia was great. We were glad Russia and the Netherlands had now landed in the same camp, opposing Germany.

Hitler had remarked, "The Russian soldier is as inferior to us as the French; the human material certainly is inferior." However, invading Russia ultimately proved to be Hitler's biggest mistake. Think of Napoleon. They miscalculated the winters. But it would be four long years before the Russian victory.

Russia never participated in The Hague convention, which regulated war conduct, and therefore was not bound by it. This gave the Germans, or so they thought, the right to massacre the prisoners of war they captured, as well as thousands of civilians. And the Russian military front would prove to be the bloodiest of the war. All told, an estimated sixteen million Russian civilians died, along with over eleven million soldiers, before they conquered Germany. Over 27 million dead, that is more then twice the entire population of my home country. No other Allied country came anywhere near those losses. The Russians deserved to be the first to arrive in Berlin at the war's end, and unfortunately for us they did just beat out the Americans.

On December 7, 1941, the Japanese attacked Pearl Harbor. America then entered the war, on both the Pacific and European fronts. My parents were overjoyed. They had the feeling the tide would turn.

The U.S. was a greater industrial power than Germany at every level. And it had the financial resources to provide vital loans to the Allies: $31 billion to Britain, $11 billion to the Soviet Union, $5 billion to China and $3 billion to thirty-five other countries. This "Lend-Lease" program allowed Allied countries to acquire war material against the promise to pay after the war's end. Had Britain attempted to sustain its military outlay from domestic resources, its economy would certainly have been broken. For Russia, the Germans had captured or destroyed most of the Ukraine, which bordered Poland, destroying its military industry, which was concentrated there. Lend-Lease money helped buy them time and resources to relocate that industry deeper within the USSR. It was in boots made in America that the Russians advanced on Germany.

But war isn't just economics; it's fighting. And initial reports after America joined the war were not encouraging. From the attack on Pearl Harbor until well into 1942, the Allies suffered continuing defeat on the battlefield, such as Guam, the Dutch Indies, and the Philippines. But finally late in 1942 they were able to start on the offense. We heard of approximately fifty percent casualties at Iwo Jima. My parents wondered if we'd ever be free again.

The Allies were supplied by ship over the Atlantic. In 1941 and 1942, German U-Boats torpedoed 2,452 merchant marine ships, as well as 175 war ships. The losses were enormous. Of the 40,900 men who sailed, 25,870 were killed. The situation for all of us became more and more precarious.

My father now had to sleep at work, to guard the supplies. One night, while peacefully asleep there, an air raid occurred. A bomb dropped in the gutter above his head, but much to our luck, failed to explode. My father was like a cat with nine lives; how fortunate he was then, as well as later.

On the first of May 1942, the Resistance called for a strike, this time because of our former soldiers having to report again. After the 5 day war, our surviving soldiers had been taken prisoners of war and later released to return home. However, now all of these men were to be taken prisoner again. Their names were printed in the newspapers, along with a warning: don't try to escape and go underground, or you, and whoever helps you, will be severely punished. But many did anyway.

Germany needed our men for its war machine. Five hundred thousand of our men had already been taken to work as slaves in German factories, where many died as the allied planes bombed the factories. I did hear stories that in the south of the country toward the German border, men were hauled out of bed in the middle of the night to be used in slave labor. As the former soldiers were young men, they were to be taken to work in the German factories; we knew this new attempt must fail!

Our underground newspapers requested for all work to be halted for one day, by the entire nation. Inexorably they started the fight with this weapon, the strike! I have no idea how many former soldiers reported, or how many went underground. Because of this strike, forty-one men were executed throughout the country, the ones that incited the strike. For that, the whole country was being punished.

Because we were troublemakers who liked our freedom, the Germans had imposed a curfew. No one was to be outside between 8 p.m. and 6 a.m. My parents were in their early thirties; the curfew must have been very hard for them. No one was to be outside on the streets except for our "friendly occupiers." And the quiet outside, we, who were used to the sounds of the tram going by, people walking and talking, people on bikes, and now there was nothing after 8 p.m.

Since practice was held at night, and was a half-hour walk, the curfew also finished my dream of becoming a ballerina. I was able to walk and dance on the tips of my toes, even without wearing the traditional toe shoes, and ruined my feet that way, something I did not realize until it was too late. I would be asked to stand on point and walk for the ladies in the grocers. If I did this, I would be given a candy bar. As such, I was always happy to give a small performance. After the war I was already too old to pursue this profession.

Ordinarily we had about fifty-five students in our school classroom. However, during the winter of 1943, we added refugees from the coastal areas, Zandvoort and surroundings. The Germans had built camouflage "pillboxes" with iron spikes and barbed wire over our beaches, so much so the remnants can still be found today. Everyone believed that the Allied troops were going to land in our coastal area instead of Normandy, as later occurred. Because of these fears, everyone living in the coastal areas had to evacuate; they had no choice. Our classroom, though already full, was now overflowing; there were kids in the most impossible places. The children from the coastal areas were displaced, but had to have schooling. Despite unbelievably cramped conditions, learn we did!

My father, being the supervisor of the Marine supplies, had a badge in order to get into work. Sometime in 1943, my father heard there was a train full of Jews going to the death camps at the central station in Amsterdam, including a kid he knew. How he got this information I do not know. The Marine headquarters were right on the water, a short walking distance from the central train station. My father, being the man he was, decided he was going to save whomever he possibly could.

He went into the train station, and found the train heavily guarded with armed soldiers. My father flashed his badge—like a very important man—announcing to the Germans that were standing besides the train that he needed three or four good strong young men to help him with whatever he dreamed up. Somehow they agreed to his request and into the train he went. Finding the young man he knew, he pointed to him and those standing beside him, "You, you, and you," and out of the train they went. He had such nerve. Once outside, they scattered to their freedom as quickly as they could. I was recently asked if I could corroborate the train story; of course I cannot. I don't even think I knew about it at the time. No one in his right mind would crow about such very dangerous things. But all of us kids know it to be the truth, and that is enough.

CHAPTER 12

Ways of Fighting Back

My father had his own ways of resisting. I have been told, "He stole the Germans blind." The truth is that he took German supplies and gave them to the Dutch, sort of like a Robin Hood.

By this time most of the Dutch Marine supplies had been confiscated, and were used by the Germans. When they ran out, they were replaced by German goods. My father managed to hang on to some of the Dutch supplies by putting them in a secret hide away It now looked that there were only German supplies left, which at that point still came in frequently (later in the war they ran out of supplies too). He stole their supplies in various clever ways—as an example, if a truck with 100 pair of sailor slacks came into the warehouse, my father would double-fold fifty pair in such a way that it looked like one hundred; the other fifty pair went out the "back door." Not really the back door, as the gateways were guarded by German soldiers. Mostly older men were used at these guard posts. But my father got the goods out in various ways.

When wheelbarrows were used to take out the trash, numerous times a day, German guards would occasionally take a look. However, they eventually became so accustomed with the trash hauling, that they rarely even looked at it any more. My father had saddlebags on his bike, which was parked outside the gate. He frequently wore a long coat, and would wrap a pair of slacks around his waist. The women of the neighborhood fared well; he either gave stuff away or traded it for something we needed. He was careful and clever, and for a long time, did not get caught;

until someone snitched on him. Eventually, he would go to prison for this.

He brought home all kinds of canned foods from the warehouse. Excellent in quality, this pocketed food kept us and many others alive. More times than I can remember, my mother sent me downstairs with a pan of food she had cooked. Both neighbors below us were hungry and loved every meal I brought them. On the first floor lived a divorcée with a son a little older than I was. The man on the second floor, despite having been knighted by our queen for his services, was scared of his own shadow. He never dared to do anything risky, even if it came to keeping his family alive. I believe it is quite possible that they would have starved if it weren't for my parents' offerings of food.

The baker came to our homes three times a week. He would ring the doorbell and we would go down to the street level to buy bread and rolls. Another man came three times a week to pick up our vegetable refuse to feed to his animals. He, too, would ring the doorbell, call out "schillenman" (refuse man) and then climb the four flights of stairs to our apartment, where he would pick up the potato peelings and such. The same happened with the vuilnisman (trash collector). He too came upstairs; he would take our large trash can, which we had set out on the landing for him, go down the stairs to empty it, and bring the can back upstairs. Talk about exercise!

Three times a week the milkman would deliver fresh milk to our door. He came before the war and during the war. I felt bad for him when he got to our house; although there were many such houses, and had no doubt many such customers. He had to walk up four flights of stairs to reach our apartment. Each flight had seventeen steps. No wonder by the time he reached our landing his nose was always dripping. He would lug a large aluminum container of raw milk. He would lift off the lid of the container and ladle milk into our milk cooker. Milk cookers were sold as part of sets of pots and pans. Everyone used them.

The ladle held one liter; our milk cooker held more than that I think. Since the milk was not pasteurized, mom had to boil the milk before we could drink it. She would boil the full two liters. After it cooled, what we did not drink stayed in the milk cooker in the cupboard. We had no refrigeration at this time. We cooked with gas, putting coins in the meter to give us enough gas to prepare our food, and if you forgot to buy those coins, you simply could not cook. While I still love milk to this day, I recall so vividly how concerned I was with each visit of the milkman. I was certain the drip of his nose would drop into our container of milk. As a young girl, it so traumatized me that even after mum had boiled the milk, I was still leery. I never dared to say anything. I was too young to realize that boiling the milk would have killed anything; yet it makes me shudder to think of his drippy nose so close to our freshly delivered milk. None of these things are done today.

CHAPTER 13

Father Imprisoned

One night in January 1943, I had a terrible nightmare. Remember, visits from the Gestapo had occurred before. I dreamt they came to arrest my father—a fear that was constantly on my mind—most likely also on my parents' minds, though they never voiced that when we children were around. I woke up and thought I saw Germans standing in the corner of my bedroom. I screamed so loud that my parents heard me downstairs. After telling my parents about my nightmare, my mother calmed me down and I went back to sleep. Little did I know then how prophetic a dream it was.

Indeed, two weeks later they arrested my father. As we were having supper, the doorbell rang and we heard them announce "Polizei" (police) from below; it was the Gestapo. We knew this was trouble. I knew what to do if they should come. They had to climb four flights of stairs, and I used that time to quickly grab anything that could get us in trouble—papers or whatever contraband—ran upstairs to the attic, and carefully hid them under our stored coal. I stayed upstairs, and did not see my father leave when they arrested him.

My mother was very distraught, as were all of us, but she was a tiger when she made up her mind to do something. The very next day she set out for the neighborhood police station. They did not know much about the situation, but through them she at least learned that he had been taken to Niewersluis, a suburb of Amsterdam. She traveled there by bus, only to learn he had already been moved to Maassluis, near Rotterdam. So she took the train to Maassluis, but they would not tell her the

64

charges against him. They absolutely would not tell her anything, nor was she permitted to see him.

For a time—I think it was three or four long weeks—we really had no clue where he was. Mom never gave up and we eventually found out he had been moved to a prison on the Weteringschans in Amsterdam. Now she could do something, bring him clean clothes, soap, a toothbrush and toothpaste, the things he really needed. Little did we know that he ate the toothpaste to quell the rumbling of his stomach.

While he was there, ten men were randomly hauled out of the prison and shot as reprisal for some high-ranking officer of the German army that had been shot by the underground. He was spared; it simply—and fortunately—was not his time.

My mother then had our family doctor write a letter stating that she had an urgent need for surgery, and that her four children would be left home alone. Armed with that letter, she went to SS headquarters in the Euterpe Straat in Amsterdam. She said she had come to talk to an officer. It was gutsy. Neither of my parents lacked guts.

The officer showed my mother a piece of paper. But she could not read German, and pretended not to understand him. The officer said, "Frau, your husband has admitted guilt." To which she replied that it was not possible; he had not done anything wrong. The officer then pointed at my father's signature on the paper, slapped his hand on the table, and screamed, "Don't you recognize his signature?" "Sure," said my mom, "I know his signature." The officer said that my father had admitted he is guilty. "No," said my mother. "How can he possibly admit to something he has not done?"

The officer tried to trick her in every way, questioning her thoroughly, over and over. We later learned the paper was a receipt for the clean clothes she had brought him, and he had signed for. My mother just knew he hadn't admitted guilt and never would, and thank goodness she wouldn't give him up. People in their fright will admit to a lot of things. She was fearless, though later said she was quavering inside.

After what seemed like hours, the officer said, "Frau, go home; your husband will be home in an hour." And to our surprise that is indeed what happened. When I came home from school, there he was—home—infested with scabies and head lice, both of which we all promptly shared. We were so happy to see him, that we had climbed all over him before we knew those details.

He told us that they tried every which way to make him talk. They got him up during the night for their interrogations; sleep deprivation was a typical tactic then as in modern warfare. Though their treatment was rough, at least they did not beat him. He learned what being hungry meant; the watery substance they fed the prisoners was not enough for any nutrition. But to them, they were only prisoners.

My mother literally got him out of the claws of the feared SS; what a feat! Her forbearers were from Austria and France, several generations prior. Her maiden name is Austrian. She was an extremely pretty lady, and that, plus having a German-sounding last name, might have played a part in this surprisingly easy, if not gutsy, rescue. However, we were also fortunate in that the fact that the charges against my father were extremely vague, which they surmised, and that the informant was the husband of one of my mother's cousins. It could have gone the other way, and I may not have ever seen my father again.

Most people were so scared of the SS that they blurted out all they knew at the first sign of trouble, to save their necks. My father, however, never revealed the names of the others that were involved. To this day, I can only respect him for that. He did not say a word and kept a young man out of prison with his silence. For many years, the parents of the young man sent my father flowers on his birthday, until the young man got on his own, and then he continued to send them himself. We then looked forward to flowers—and a freshly baked torte from the young man he rescued from the death camps. He had become a fine pastry chef!

CHAPTER 14

Life Goes On

Although it would get much worse later on, we were beginning to know hunger in 1943. Hermann Goering threatened that if it came to food shortages, it would not be the German population who would suffer but the people of the occupied countries. At school they were giving us vitamin C tablets, trying to make up for the fact that fresh fruits and vegetables were being shipped to enemy territory. Indeed, the Netherlands (or Holland if you wish) was held close to the level of minimum sustenance. People were becoming extremely thin, and began eating the most improbable things.

The health of the Dutch population was deteriorating fast. The increase in people with tuberculosis was frightening. Collectively, several hundred doctors sent a letter of protest to Seyss-Inquart, head of the national government. Seyss-Inquart's reaction to the letter was, "How dare they?" He sent his police and imprisoned the doctors. This was to demonstrate who was in charge. After a few days, he released them and let them return home.

By this time, the Germans had stolen all our manufacturing machinery, which they had moved to their country. With no more equipment for manufacturing, there was nothing to be bought in the stores: little or no food, no shoes, and no clothing. I was 5' 7" tall at age twelve, the tallest kid in my class, and a real beanstalk at just eighty pounds. My mother made me a dress out of two of hers and knitted my sister and me sweaters out of leftover yarn. When I outgrew my winter coat, there was no longer a simple solution.

My father brought home some heavy gray wool pieces that had been previously used to insulate barrels. These were not yard goods, but just several pieces of heavy cloth. My parents took me to a tailor, who for a lot of money managed to make a winter coat out of the material. Although it was warm, it was the most uncomfortable, unappealing thing I ever wore. It had absolutely no pizzazz! Since I learned to sew at a young age, I later wondered if a seamstress rather than a tailor had made it, it could have been made more appealing. What difference might have come from the touch of a woman—knowing what a young girl would want? All I had then was a coat made with material so stiff I could hardly move my arms in the contraption.

My parents, feeling my distress, tried to pacify me by giving me a navy blue hat which they had acquired by trading a sheet with someone. It was common to get things by swapping, trading, and a lot of finagling. It was a felt hat, which Mom called a Deanna Durbin hat, named for an internationally famous movie star of the 1930s and 1940s. It looked good on me, and I felt oh so beautiful in it, which was the whole idea in the first place. Such smart parents I had!

There were no more shoes, so we wore sort of a wooden clog with a strap. Our school had a wooden stairway. The noise of us kids going up and down the stairs was so deafening, our principal threw a fit. Well, perhaps some of us clumped a little too hard on purpose. My father re-soled our shoes endlessly. Anything he could find he used for soles, such as the leather sheath used to carry a knife. He was no cobbler, but did a remarkably fine job. My father would apply hot wax on the seams and all edges of our shoes. It not only helped make them more durable, but given the cheap and sometimes awful colored materials he had to make our news soles from, it made them look a bit more luxurious, as well.

Remember, whatever shoes we had throughout the war were rationed as well. We got one pair a year, and they had to last. Each year, my father took me with my ration coupon to a store where I bought a pair of shoes; nothing fancy, believe me. I have very narrow feet, and that made it even more difficult One year, we went shoe shopping on a Saturday morning, and on Monday morning it was raining. We had a half hour walk to school, and by the time I got there, the shoes had fallen apart. They were made of pressed cardboard or something similarly flimsy. There went my shoe ration for the whole year. There was absolutely not a shoe to be had. I envisioned a year without a real pair of shoes. My father, however, came through as usual. He managed to bring me a pair of soldiers shoes. They were ugly, and I don't remember how well they fit, but they kept my feet dry.

In the summer of 1943, we were on vacation in Bussem, when suddenly my father developed seizures. I remember being very frightened; it was a scary event to witness. He had to go to the hospital. This happened a time or two after that as well.

In September of 1943, I transferred to an all-girl school to learn home economics, among other subjects. No sooner had we settled into a regular class schedule than Seyss-Inquart decided we must learn the enemy's language. Our instructor was Mrs. Franchimon. A group of us put our heads together and decided we were not going to learn their language; it was our way of resisting. When the hour was upon us, most of us students got up and announced our intentions.

Though we kept this up for six weeks, eventually they sent in an armed soldier to force us to obey. The only thing left to me was to simply not do the homework, which I fiercely avoided. Poor Mrs. Franchimon had a nervous breakdown because of us. Of course, we did not think of the results of our actions; children of thirteen do not typically think of such things.

My best friend in school was Mary, also thirteen years old. She was cute, with brown wavy hair, quite well developed, and striking in appearance. She went on dates with German soldiers. One day I was called into the principal's office and warned not to hang out with Mary any longer, because she was dating the enemy. And much to my regret, I could no longer be her friend. It was considered aiding the enemy.

When I say "soldier," it may prompt an image of a thirteen year-old dating a twenty-five year-old; but that was not the case. The soldiers she dated were more likely sixteen or seventeen years of age. Hitler was running out of men and was drafting sixteen-year-olds, as a solution. As the war progressed, the soldiers we saw were only youngsters and old men, except for the ferocious SS, the Dutch Brigade of the Waffen SS and the Proletarians of the NSB. They were still enough for us to worry about.

On the occasion of my fourteenth birthday, one of my aunts brought me an apple torte. Being a kid, I did not appreciate it and was less than thrilled. I suppose I was looking for another sort of gift. It is only now, looking back at the times, that I realize how special a gift it truly was.

My mother had helped to keep the youth theater running during the early years of the war, but by the winter of 1944, it too had stopped. There obviously were more pressing needs. As the war continued, I no longer studied dance. One of my older cousins recently told me I used to tap dance for her; something I do not remember. My mother and I did have a chance to perform again after the war ended. We were both in plays and attended fancy balls after the performances.

I took ballroom dancing and danced a lot. Maybe I danced too well for my own good, as the instructor would beg me to help him out by dancing with those who needed the best partners to make up for their own lack of skills. My dance skills were amazing for this girl who started out needing surgery to walk soon after I was born.

During wartime, I had cooking lessons in school. Everything we used was pre-measured. Some girls, including me, were so hungry we tried to eat pieces of butter or whatever they could possibly eat if the teacher was not looking, though she watched us all very carefully, as if in anticipation of catching someone. The cooking lessons really did not amount to a hill of beans. There was little to work with. I do, however, remember making mashed potatoes. Whatever we produced was sent to hospitals, because there was not much to eat there either.

My parents befriended the green grocer around the corner, and through a lot of bartering we still had access to some vegetables and potatoes. And although city slickers, somehow my mother learned how to preserve things. In the attic we had a barrel of sauerkraut, French sliced beans and green beans. We had gotten a bushel of apples, which my sister and I peeled and peeled, then cored. Mom sliced them, and we strung the apple slices to dry, hanging them in our bedroom. It worked! I can't help but think of that when I buy dried fruit. Ask me; I know how to do those things without electricity!

My best friend in the neighborhood was Annie Dekker. More than once I went to Annie's house to play, and too often stayed just past the 8 p.m. curfew. I then had to duck from doorway to doorway to get home, which usually went all right, though I was tempting fate, and now cannot think what possessed me to do that. However, just a week or two before the end of the war, there was a raid and the German squads were right in front of my parents' house when I was coming home. I could not get in until they moved on. I realize now, had I been caught, I could have been shot. But surviving the scare, at that time, I felt invincible.

My mother seemed fearless. Upon seeing a couple of SS officers walking past our front door, she spat on the ground in front of their feet. They knew why and what she was doing; where upon one of them grabbed her by the collar and suggested forcefully, "I would not do that again if I were you."

* * *

A handgun fits nicely in a hollowed-out book. Historically, Holland is not a country in which people carried guns. But during the war, things were very different. The Dutch underground needed weapons; delivered to us from the British through weapons drops. These were very dangerous undertakings. They also had to be hidden. And so, small arms were kept in hollowed-out books, and were put into bookcases alongside other books. No one ever thought to look there for guns.

Similarly, cameras had to be hidden. To be caught photographing the German bunkers one was certain to have been shot and killed. Since there was no leather available, lady's purses were made from coarse woven straw, which in turn could hide the lens of a camera. This was a somewhat safe way to photo-

71

graph the German defense bunkers; but extremely dangerous, too. Frequently, young unmarried women would risk taking such photographs. Often dressed in uniforms, such as nurses, even nuns, these young women would carry their large straw bags, their camera lens facing outward, steadily resting against the open weave. My family did not own a camera until well after the war. I had not heard about these things at the time; but as an adult I saw a photo of such a purse in a book for the first time.

Meanwhile, my father continued to have seizures and had to go to the hospital again. He shared the hospital room with Mr. Englander, an elderly man of German decent. There was no food in the hospital, so my mother walked there on a daily basis to take care of both men's needs. My father got to know Mr. Englander very well during his stay, and it appears Mr. Englander trusted my father enough to ask for his help. He knew of a German deserter who needed to find a hiding place. The man's name was Hans Gall. He had been drafted into Hitler's army but saw no sense in fighting. He therefore just walked across the border into the Netherlands, and then on to Amsterdam, where it appears he knew Mr. Englander. He arrived with hopes of finding someone who would offer him shelter. My father, not surprisingly, extended it to him. When Hans came out of hiding, at war's end, he remained a friend of my parents. He never returned to his home country.

From the start of the occupation, we were not supposed to receive any news except the Dutch censored news. The Germans had requisitioned our radios. Many people were scared and took them to the flat-bottomed boat which was the collection place, in the river Amstel. My parents were not about to turn in our radio, or anything else for that matter. There were now many articles the enemy "requisitioned."

As described earlier, our apartment had three rooms adjoining each other with wooden sliding doors. My father discovered a hollow opening on top of the closet door which was next to the sliding doors. He tapped all around and listened, then found a hollow place in which he hid our radio. Now we could carefully listen clandestinely to the BBC broadcast, which started with the first bars from Beethoven's Fifth Symphony, which has the same rhythm—tick, tick, tick, and a long tone—as the Morse code "V," which meant victory. I don't know Morse code, but have been told that this is fact.

One day the BBC announced that a very important message would be broadcast after midnight; my father stayed up to listen. We thought we would get news about the Allied invasion. Alas, it was not so. We heard the announcement that during the night Europe would be covered with V signs. Everybody was deeply disappointed that the message was not as expected, but especially that the English had so little understanding of the situation we were in. However, this incident gave Joseph Goebbels the idea to use the V for victory on his placards, and we saw it everywhere after that. The Third Reich won again, even in this minute little way.

In addition to radios, all metals such as copper, tin and lead had been requisitioned by the Germans for war manufacturing, as well as rubber, which I mentioned earlier. My parents had taken the rubber tires off our bicycles, but hid them, rather than turn them in. When I speak of tireless bikes, it means the wheels had no rubber left on them, just rims. Later there came a directive to bring in our bikes as well. After that was a directive that we had to bring in copper, bronze, and any other kind of metal that Hitler could use for his war machine. My family did not obey.

My parents had some beautiful metal items, like a set of copper Indonesian vases, as well as a bronze clock set with matching vases. Rather than turn them in, my father hid them under the floor boards, with such care that he could not find them later. If the building were being demolished today, I bet someone would find them still there. At least they were not turned into cannons!

There were terrible air battles, and sleep was becoming increasingly difficult because of the anti-aircraft cannons. On a Sunday afternoon in the winter of 1943, my parents were out, and I was babysitting. I heard the wailing of the air raid sirens. This happened frequently. Whenever planes approached the Dutch coastline, they turned on the sirens. To this day the sounds of any kind of sirens spook me. I made sure my younger sister and brothers had their winter coats on, their dog tags, ID papers, and ration cards in their pockets, and I positioned them in the stairway. I went back into the living room to literally see bombs sailing by. They fell all around, but missed us, another misdirected bomb drop. Apparently they were aiming for Euterpe Straat (street) and SS headquarters and missed.

After Dutch Marine supplies were confiscated, my father's warehouse was filled with German supplies, except for some Dutch sheets, blankets and canned food that he hid in a separate storage area. But there was the informant, who gave up the secret of the hidden Dutch supplies. Of course, the Germans wanted those, too; they wanted all we had.

My father still wouldn't give up and give it all to the Germans. By the time their trucks showed up, he had passed word around the neighborhood about the supplies leaving. The Marine barracks were on the north side of Amsterdam, in the poorest section of town. For every two bales my father threw in the enemy's truck, one bale went out of the window, where women from the neighborhood made off with it. He gave away as much as he possibly could, and I'm sure helped many that way; anything was better than to let the enemy have it.

Citizens were required to turn in their money, but especially 500 and 1,000-gulden notes, to be converted to different money. Not that we had that much money, but there were people who did—black money, made by profiteers. However, if they turned in that kind of money, they would have to account for how they got it. So in a kind of money laundering process, in order to remain safe, people converted their incriminating bank notes to gold and diamonds. When we traded in our money, I accidentally left two one-gulden notes in my wallet; I still have them.

I had some relatives who were asked by very wealthy Jewish people to be the keepers of their securities, beautiful jewelry, many diamonds, as well as some furniture. I guess the temptation was too great. They lived for years off the money they got for the Jewish belongings. I don't know how they could live with themselves after the war, knowing what they had done; but they did, and lived "well" from someone else's money. I found this despicable, as did my parents. However, I still take some comfort in knowing that the bank credits of killed Dutch Jews are subjects of trials to this day.

It was during this time that I contracted scarlet fever. It was not possible to be hospitalized at that time, so my mother did her best to isolate me in the house from the others. Despite her efforts, all of my siblings, which now included the youngest, Johnny, age four, also came down with scarlet fever. Fortunately, we all survived.

We were hearing stories about death camps regularly, including stories of people being gassed to death. If we in the Netherlands heard this, how was it is possible the German population did not?

"Uncle Max," the Jewish journalist married to my mother's friend, our piano teacher, had been arrested and sent to Vught, a concentration camp in the southern part of the Netherlands. One night in early 1943, 1,600 Jewish children from camp Vught, ages one month to fifteen years, were transported in cattle cars. Like Westerbork, Vught was sort of a staging area from which people were transferred to a death camp. Uncle Max remained in Vught until the end of the war, married to a Gentile which kept him alive but not until they had made sure he would be unable to produce offspring. Along with numerous others, he was given a vasectomy just as Jewish women were given tubal ligations to prevent them from conceiving.

CHAPTER 15

Clever Evasions

Germany was running short of manpower at home. I remember the slogans they tried at first to entice our people: "Come to work in Germany, plenty of money to be made." And when that was unsuccessful, they forced laborers from occupied lands, including the Netherlands, to go to Germany. Every man between eighteen and forty-five was obliged to work in German factories. The laborers gave half-hearted service at best, persisting in sabotage.

Some were kept in the Netherlands but forced to work on German projects, such as building the Atlantic Wall, a gigantic defense line along the entire European coast from southern France up past the Netherlands to Denmark. It was a huge project, at times requiring entire towns to be evacuated. Overall, an estimated twenty thousand houses were cleared, and 65,000 people were forced to move. Here too the Dutch workers used passive resistance, working slowly, or doing such a bad job that a task had to be redone, delaying the project's completion.

Mr. Peters, the husband of one of the leaders of the youth group, was picked up and sent to Germany; he never came back. With the air raids going on, the British, Americans or whoever dropped the bombs did not know there were Dutch, Belgian, French, Polish and Russian laborers working in the factories that they bombed, many of whom perished.

When our laborers would not agree to go to work in Germany, the employers had to make lists of how many men they had employed, after which the Dutch SS combed through the records and determined who was to be sent to Germany.

Two of my cousins found ways to escape this fate. Karel and Tim are roughly ten and seven years older than I am. They are brothers, the sons of my father's oldest sister. Tim looked like the typical Hitler dream-man: handsome, with blue eyes and wavy blond hair. He avoided being picked up by enrolling in a military school, where he was being trained to be a naval officer. Of course, the Germans thought he'd be a U-boat captain someday. However, year after year he failed most of his tests. No, dumb he was not; in fact, after the war he graduated from the naval college with high honors, but this was how he stretched out his safety.

In the winter of 1944-45, schools, including military schools, were often canceled. Tim faced grave danger, and with constant raids going on, another way had to be found. My Uncle Dirk, his father, a very handy craftsman, remodeled a closet so that Tim could disappear behind a second wall if necessary, should there be an assault squad looking for him. Thank God it was never put to use.

Even more dramatic is the story of cousin Karel. When he feared they were going to grab him, he inflicted a wound in one of his feet, and put sugar on the wound so that it became terribly infected and would not heal. This worked for a while, but he could not keep it up forever. With the wound on his foot finally closed, he needed a hiding place, which he found in Stautenburg.

There he hid at a farm in the country near Amersfoort. The young farmer and his wife had one child, around age six. They already had hidden two other men. One day they were found out, and the Dutch SS came and lined all three men up against a wall, ready to execute them. However, the farmer offered them a bribe of butter, cheese and milk. They took the bribe and the three men, as well as the farm family, were spared.

After this, another hiding place had to be found. My Uncle Harry owned a very large villa in Amersfoort, which had been requisitioned by the enemy, to house a group of German nurses. It was so large it was heated by a boiler. My cousin then became employed as the maintenance man. There was no pay, but it was the perfect hiding place, right under the enemy's nose. It lasted until the final few weeks of the war.

As the war went on, the demand was not just for factory workers. In early 1944, I unwittingly witnessed how forced military enlistment works. School was never in session on Wednesday afternoons, and with my parents' permission I went to visit my aunt and cousins, Tim and Karel's family, in a suburb on the far eastern side of the city. At this time, trams were still running.

I had to change trams to get there, and as I stood waiting for Tram Number 9 to come, suddenly several German assault squads rushed along. It was a busy time of day, with many people coming home from work on their bicycles. The Germans grabbed all the men they saw. One man tried to make a run for it and was shot.

I didn't understand it at the time, but later learned that Hitler was so short on manpower, he used this type of forced enlistment of unwilling Dutch men into his army to fight in Russia on the Eastern Front. I have no idea how many of these conscripted men died while fighting "for" Hitler, and their names remain unknown. I am quite certain he did the same in the other occupied countries, as I later learned when a conscripted Russian managed to escape in the Netherlands. It was not that Russia had ever been completely occupied like we were, but Hitler's armies had been there in some parts. Had I been a boy, they would have grabbed me too that day.

CHAPTER 16

D-Day and Beyond

Field Marshal Gerd von Rundstedt was The Reich's most distinguished army officer. He and Hitler had never agreed on how to meet the threat of the oncoming Allied forces. Before the Normandy invasion, appealing for reinforcements, Rundstedt had bluntly informed the Führer's headquarters that the Western Allies, superior in men, equipment and planes, could land anywhere they wanted. Hitler disagreed, and boasted that the almost three thousand mile fortifications along the European coastline, built in part by forced Dutch labor, would make the coast impregnable.

Second in command was the much younger Erwin Rommel, also a field marshal. There were very few things on which von Rundstedt and Rommel saw eye to eye. Rommel believed that Allied landing forces should be stopped at the beaches, while von Rundstedt believed the invaders should be wiped out after they had landed. Their one point of agreement was that the Führer's over-confidence was appalling.

At one point, while writing this book, I realized it was June 6, 2006, which made it sixty-two years ago to the day that the troops had landed in Normandy, France, not on the Dutch coastline, as was expected for many years. It was a day of great reflection for me.

Through mid-1944, Britain was turned into one huge military base, with nearly three million members of the Allied forces gathered in southern England. Yet the utmost secrecy about the invasion was kept. The German military did not know where the strike would come, other than it would be in France. In fact, they had been fed the wrong information and were encouraged by the Allies to believe the landings would take place at Calais, the shortest distance across the English Channel.

The Germans were so sure the Allies would never risk an amphibious assault from the wide crossing to Normandy, that when the invasion began, they first thought it was a mere diversionary tactic. Another factor in the victory is that in the months before D-Day, Allied air forces dropped a staggering 200,000 tons of bombs on French targets, damaging Germany's ability to reinforce the beaches.

On June 6, 1944, commencing at 6:30 a.m., 75,000 British and Canadian troops, and 57,000 US troops, landed on Normandy beaches from nearly seven thousand ships and landing craft. Despite Rommel's brilliant improvisations, and despite suffering severe losses, Allied troops breached the so-called impregnable wall in less than eighteen hours. Impregnable? Humbug. We learned that nothing is virtually impregnable. Thank goodness it was not!

We wanted to hear the real news about D-Day, not the German version. Therefore, my father cut the wallpaper to expose the hollow above the door where our radio was hidden. We had to take a stepladder to listen to the BBC; my father listened first, then mom, or if she could not, as the oldest daughter, I would listen. Sometimes other family members, like my Grandfather Herman came to listen, and perhaps also to get a meal.

In the wake of D-Day, Hitler had no intention of conceding victory to the Allies, even though the Third Reich, which he had boasted would last a millennium, was tottering. Yet each move he made seemed more desperate than the last. But I, for one, am glad he would not listen to his generals; after all, he had never made it any further than corporal, but thought he knew best.

In August, Walter Model was named commander-in-chief west to replace Gunther von Kluge, who had committed suicide out of pure desperation. A letter from von Kluge, delivered to the Führer, basically stated, "We told you so." He and the other commanders in the west predicted this would happen and were ignored. The letter concluded by pleading with Hitler to be great enough to end the horribly hopeless situation they were in.

But Hitler would not listen. Rommel was badly wounded by Allied strafing in July of 1944, and no one had been sent to replace him. Confident that he could right the situation, Model took on Rommel's job as commander-in-chief of Army Group B, as well as commander of the Western Front. It appeared that despite Model's expertise, however, the task he faced was almost impossible to accomplish. Army Group B was battling for survival at the border of Belgium and Luxembourg to our south. Allied armor had torn a 75-mile gap in Model's line, running between Belgium and its northern neighbor—us, the Netherlands. The Allies had already made great progress sweeping north through France and liberating it. Unless the Germans closed the gap, the Allies could press north through the Netherlands and into northwest Germany.

Model's other immediate concern was the Belgian deep-water port of Antwerp, which had just been captured by the British, its port facilities intact. However, the Allies needed to clear the water approaches to this great inland port in order to use it for shipping. The Allies' obstacle was the estuary of the Scheldt River, which connects Antwerp to the North Sea, and was controlled by a relatively small number of German troops.

Allied forces were nearby. Model was a skilled tactician, known for his defensive skills. He understood the importance of stopping the Allies, not just in their advance to the north, but from opening Antwerp as a supply line. He knew that in the area south of the Scheldt was General von Zangen's 15th Army of over 80,000 men.

On the afternoon of September 4, at Army Group B's headquarters, Model issued a series of orders. He commanded von Zangen to hold at all costs the southern bank of the Scheldt River. With the remainder of his troops, von Zangen was to attack northeast into the troops of the Canadians and Royal Marines. The measure was desperate, but if the attack was successful, it might stop the British forces in Antwerp.

Knowing the high stakes, Model pleaded with Hitler for three days to get reinforcements. What he got instead was a demotion. von Kluge had lasted forty-four days as commander-in-chief west, and Model just eighteen days. He was then replaced by Field Marshal Gerd von Rundstedt. Hitler, from his headquarters in Rustenburg, East Prussia, which he had named Wolf's Lair, called von Rundstedt out of his forced "retirement." The man had been fired, not shot to death like many others, just two months earlier. An unknowing scapegoat for Hitler's faulty strategies at D-Day, he was suddenly called back to the war's western front.

Although Hitler detested von Rundstedt, he was smart enough to recognize him as a most able commander, well-respected by the troops. He was indeed successful in quickly regrouping the fragmented German forces in the area, preparing them to face the advance of reportedly massive Allied forces. As to Model's other concern—defending the Scheldt estuary—even von Rundstedt eventually proved inadequate to the task.

At the time he was replaced, what mattered to Model—and eventually to the Dutch—was that he could at last concentrate on being a front line commander, the head of Army Group B; it was what he knew best. One order he issued on his last day as commander-in-chief west proved to be momentous—the relocation of two badly weakened SS Panzer corps to a quiet rural area which included the Dutch city of Arnhem and the village of Oosterbeek.

The name of the lieutenant general of the Panzer corps was Bittrich. His orders were to supervise the refitting of his 9th and 10th Panzer divisions. Little did he know what role his divisions would play in the next two weeks, having a long-term and devastating impact on the war-weary Dutch.

My father came home with a lot of things obtained on the black market. Trying to clothe a family of six was not an easy task. Stores were devoid of things to buy; materials, machinery and other supplies had been transported long ago to enemy territory.

On or around March 11, 1944, my father came home with an enormous suitcase full of clothing. Even though it was used merchandise, to us this clothing was like gold. How fortunate we felt; yet we could almost predict what would happen next with the traitors across the street.

March 13, 1944, was my aunt's birthday. Going to see her at night was impossible because of the curfew. My mother and grandmother, wanting to visit for her special day, went to see her in the afternoon, which left me home alone. I believe I was home from school due to a cold.

The doorbell rang. Since we were four flights of stairs up, I had no way of knowing for sure who was coming up the stairs; though due to the heavy footsteps I had a fair idea. Sure enough, a police visit once again.

The offending suitcase was clearly visible standing in my parents' bedroom. The officers told me they were acting on a report that we had a large amount of contraband at the house. I knew full well there were sailor pants hidden behind the second door of my parents' large wardrobe. So, full of youthful bravado, I opened up the first door of the closet, with nothing more than our clothing to be seen there. They never asked me to open the second door, and I did not volunteer. Nor did they ask what was in the suitcase. Could this have been another example of "good" Dutch Policemen? I'll never know for sure, but I like to think so.

CHAPTER 17

The End Is Near, but Not Here

In early September 1944, the Allied troops had freed not only the Belgian cities of Brussels and Antwerp, but Maastricht, a large city in the south of the Netherlands. Rumors were flying that Breda, another southern city, was freed as well, which unfortunately proved to be false.

The Dutch government had not wanted to use the "Old Water Line," a defensive line allowing land to be flooded to slow down advancing armies, as generations before them had. As such, the Germans could not flood us as they would have been able to in the past. The "New Water Line," which was updated and extended, then contained many of our large cities. When the Allies invaded our country, Antwerp had already been freed. However, the island of Walcheren was still occupied by a large number of German forces, determined to hang on to this very important supply port to the city. Fighting was so fierce that it made a landing like that in Normandy impossible. The Allied forces responded by bombing the dykes to flood the island. Though the Allies had warned the citizens with pamphlets, 180 inhabitants of Westkapelle died. To my knowledge, no one perished in the other two towns that were flooded.

It was utter confusion. In Amsterdam, my home town, the atmosphere was really tense. My father's office closed, as did many others, including our stock exchange. The high command of the Dutch underground felt uneasy in their secret meeting, tensely watching the situation. The Resistance leaders knew the Germans had virtually no fighting forces left in the Netherlands that were capable of stopping a large Allied drive—only an undermanned division of old men guarding coastal defenses, where they had been sitting since 1940 without ever firing a shot.

The frantic flight of the Dutch Nazis and German citizens, such as the nurses who had occupied my Uncle Harry's villa, had been triggered by Seyss-Inquart and by the brutal NSB leader, Anton Mussert. They had become nervous after watching the fate of the Germans in France and Belgium, and on September 1, had ordered all German citizens to the east side of the Netherlands, closer to the German border. Seyss-Inquart and Mussert were among the first to leave.

At first, most of the Germans, as well as the traitorous Dutch civilians, moved at a rather leisurely pace. But after the British captured Brussels and Antwerp, bringing Allied tanks very close to the Dutch border, panic ensued among the Nazis.

On September 3, Queen Wilhelmina told her people in a broadcast on the clandestine BBC radio from London that liberation was at hand! She also announced that Prince Bernhard had become commander in chief of the Dutch forces, and would assume leadership of the underground resistance groups.

The prince followed with an announcement of his own. He asked the underground to have armbands ready that displayed in distinct letters the word "Oranje," the royal family's surname, but not to display them without his orders.

A broadcast message then came from General Eisenhower, commander of the Allied forces, confirming that liberation was imminent. Within a few hours, these broadcasts were followed by the prime minister of the Dutch government, Pieter Gerbrandy. He stated that the Allied armies had crossed the Dutch border, and urged us to warmly welcome them.

We were hysterical with joy, and on September 5, I was one of thousands who walked for miles out of town to greet our liberators. I remember the rumors around me—they are here, they are there—but no one came! And after waiting for hours, I desolately walked back home.

This day was called Dolle Dinsdag, which translates as "Crazy Tuesday" or "Mad Tuesday." While we rejoiced at the thought of being liberated, the Allied activity created severe panic amongst the enemy and their compatriots. The traitorous Dutch Nazis, including mayors and officials appointed by the Nazis, numbered about fifty thousand. Before bolting, they made a run on the banks, to close accounts and empty safe deposit boxes. They then fled for their lives as quickly as they could, on anything they could find. Trains to Germany were filled to capacity; even barges on the Rhine River were filled with fleeing people, carrying as many of their possessions as they possibly could.

Hour after hour the traffic mounted. So desperate were they to reach safety that they ignored the blackout rules, and ran trucks with headlights blazing. The German officers seemed to have lost control over their men. Everywhere soldiers tried to desert. In their haste to escape, they stole bikes, horses, cars, and wagons, and even ordered farmers at gunpoint to haul them to Germany.

Some fleeing troops pushed hand carts piled high with loot filched from the Netherlands, France, Belgium, and Luxembourg. Along the way they tried selling the stolen items. Among the retreating soldiers there was no shortage of alcohol, either. They moved large quantities of wine and liquor in horse-drawn carts. One soldier jumping off a truck proved to be a Russian who had been conscripted into the Wehrmacht, just like they did with all the men I saw being picked up while waiting for my tram that day.

We thought for sure that the war would be over in a matter of days. Suddenly the Dutch flag appeared everywhere, along with cheering crowds. I remember people singing the Dutch national anthem. Enterprising merchants sold orange buttons, and small red, white and blue lapel pins; I still have mine bought for a quarter in the bookstore next door to us. But this all proved to be premature, a false alarm. Our liberation was not at hand. It would take another eight months. The worst was yet to come.

The retreat out of the Netherlands was slowing, although few of us realized this yet. Roads were still choked, but there was a difference in the movement. German troops entering Arnhem from the west were not moving eastward into Germany. It became clear that this was not a temporary stay; they were regrouping. We wondered if the optimistic broadcasts from London were false. My father tried to figure it out; he thought they were a cruel hoax. If the British had indeed taken major cities to our south, which we believed to be true, then surely it would not stop there. We could not be forgotten; but we were. We had been abandoned!

CHAPTER 18

Operation Market-Garden

A fter D-Day in June, there were high hopes the war could be ended in 1944. Given the successful liberation of France, and strong Allied advances in Belgium, it seemed the Netherlands might have been liberated with ease those first days of September. Instead it was about to become a vast battlefield of the western front. Meanwhile, back in my home town, we had no idea what was going on. We had to go back to school as usual.

Our queen ordered the railroad workers to go on strike, and most of them gladly complied. It had already become increasingly dangerous on the trains because of the constant strafing. Sabotage and reprisals occurred daily. My widowed future-mother-in-law and her family sheltered a railroad worker after the queen ordered a strike. Of course, this was very dangerous; however, they managed to hide the man until the end of the war.

Given the panicked exodus of Germans in those early days of September, we thought we would soon be rid of them all. But Hitler was not giving up so easily. Along our southern border, German military police were closing off roads leading to Germany, to stop the flight of German soldiers. In Eindhoven, which is close to the Belgian border, the retreat had already stopped.

Even more discouraging was the discovery that fresh German troops were arriving by train. They unloaded quickly, and set out for the Belgian-Dutch border, where they were soon digging in along the north side of Belgium's Albert Canal, almost one hundred miles long, just south of the border. This eighty-foot-wide, deep-cut water barrier was the new German front line left by Model, and placed under the command of airborne pioneer General Kurt Student. He had led the air attack on Holland in 1940, and was now back, calling in his three thousand paratroopers, who had scattered across the Reich. They were probably the only combat-ready reserve forces in Germany at the time. He combined them with miscellaneous service troops in the area to form what was euphemistically called the "First Parachute Army"—oddly, paratroopers with no planes.

Upon his arrival at Albert Canal, Student was appalled to see that defense positions had not been prepared—no trenches or fortifications. Finding all bridges over the canal still intact, another critical task was to have demolition charges placed to destroy the crossings. Before long, Student had organized some semblance of a defensive line. Although this patchwork of men was too sparse to close the seventy-five-mile gap from Antwerp to the Dutch border, they were to make a big difference in the outcome of the Allies' next major offensive.

In addition, on September 6, we heard about a serious mistake the British had made, failing to cut the escape route from Belgium of eighty-six thousand German troops, who were now regrouping in the south of our country. Remember, there were still those SS Panzer divisions being refitted and trained in the country near Arnhem.

While the Germans quietly regrouped and stabilized their Western forces, the Allies were engaged in a strategic debate at the highest levels of command in Europe. On one side was General Eisenhower's "broad front" strategy, advancing everywhere, as decided upon before D-Day. On the other side was British General Montgomery's preference to identify German weak spots and make focused thrusts through them.

Of key importance was how to resolve logistical supply issues that were halting Allied advances. The liberation of Paris on August 25 ended the Normandy campaign, but the Allies were still dependent on the shallow docks built on the original invasion beaches and the nearby deep-water port of Cherbourg. Other important ports on the Channel Coast, such as Dunkirk, would remain in German hands until the war's end. Although over-the-beach supply operations performed well, and enough supplies reached the continent to serve Allied needs, a short-age of transportation to move these supplies forward created a bottleneck.

At the beginning of September, Cherbourg had 70,000 tons of stockpiled supplies, but lacked sufficient train and truck transport to distribute them. A makeshift trucking operation called Red Ball Express was of some help, but couldn't solve the larger problem.

Eisenhower knew they needed a port closer to the front, and Antwerp was the only port in Allied hands. He wanted to pri-oritize the broad Allied advance through Belgium, stopping at Antwerp just long enough to make the port operational. But he was also under pressure to get the reorganized Allied Airborne forces involved in the war, and the plan proposed by Montgom-ery and his supporters relied heavily on the airborne army. The plan would also isolate the V-2 rocket launch sites that were bombarding London. In a change of mind, Eisenhower gave a green light for Montgomery's plan, as long as it was done quickly, so as not to give the Germans more time to rebuild their forces.

So where were the German weak points and what was this plan? The River Rhine was the last great natural defensive barrier of Germany on the west. The key weak point was the Netherlands, which had been under German occupation for four years, and German forces there were seen as especially inef-fective. The narrow thrust would be through the Dutch city of Arnhem, where the Rhine River crossed into the Netherlands, just north of the Germans' 400 mile west wall defense, known as the Siegfried Line, gaining access into the German industrial heartland.

The plan was called "Operation Market-Garden." To this day it was the largest airborne drop in military history. Three Allied divisions would be involved, landing from south to north. The US 101st Airborne would drop on Eindhoven and take the canal crossings at Veghel. The US 82nd Airborne would land on bridges over the Maas and Waal Rivers at Nijmegen. And the British 1st Airborne, then later the Polish 1st Parachute Brigade, would be dropped on the Rhine Bridge at Arnhem. This was the "Market" plan.

In the "Garden" phase, British General Horrocks' 30 Corps would spearhead a rapid advance northward along the Eindhoven-Nijmegen-Arnhem Road, linking the three airborne divisions and securing their river crossings, arriving at Arnhem on day three to relieve the paratroopers there. The US 1st Army would join the Arnhem forces in a pincer movement from the southwest, and all would complete the push into Germany and on to Berlin. If only it were as simple as it sounded.

The Airborne units had suffered heavily in the prior campaign—forty percent losses in forty days of fighting—and were still reorganizing in their camps in England when the orders came down. Yet they were the greatest airborne force the world has ever seen—highly motivated, superbly armed and confident they could do the job, if 30 Corps could relieve them as planned. But there were serious obstacles from the outset that threatened that plan.

Overriding it all was the fact that key planning tasks were done badly or not at all. This problem ran from the highest level at headquarters, down to the detailed planning and leadership required at the small unit level. Heroism was no match for bad choices and opportunities ignored, such as help from local resistance workers. Then again, it was all planned in a week, compared to months for the Normandy invasion.

Also critical was the underestimation of German military strength in the Netherlands. In reality, Model's Army Group B would be ready and able to perform admirably. The German 15th Army were assumed to be fleeing the Canadians at Antwerp, but had in fact regrouped into an effective fighting force in our south. And the SS Panzer divisions near Arnhem obviously played a key role. General Student's return as commander of the German Airborne forces brought with him important prior knowledge of the area, and his air support did much to delay the advance of 30 Corps so critical to the operation.

Drop zone selection was often poor, particularly at Arnhem, where command inexperience led to drops ten miles from the bridge. This was determined based on a perception that enemy flak from the city and nearby airfield would threaten paratroopers or towing gliders in that air space. It's hard to imagine that with the element of surprise this would have led to more damage than the ultimate results of dropping so far from the target.

Due to a lack of aircraft, drops had to be spread out over several days—so much for the element of surprise—and first arrivals had to defend the drop zones for the next rounds. Spread-out drops of weapons and supplies meant some were dropped in zones that were by then overrun by the enemy. Communication problems were rife, contributing to inability to redirect supply planes.

Last but not least, there was Highway 69, the only road the armored formations would use. It was a two-lane, typical Dutch dike-like road, with low-lying soft soil on either side that could not support tanks. All told, it was not conducive to the three-day transit called for in the plan.

This is how it actually happened:

Day 1, Sunday, September 17, 1944: The drops began in daylight and on target. Approximately 14,000 airplanes left the southern part of England, consisting of American, British, and Polish troops. Those paratroopers were to land around Arnhem, the birthplace of my future husband. The English thought that the German troops were demoralized, after their heavy losses in France and that the operation would be a piece of cake—how wrong they were.

The Dutch population near the three drop zones, watched from their rooftops, confident that they were about to be liberated. That day the first-dropped US 101st and 82nd Airborne met most of their goals, capturing six of seven assigned bridges. Only the Son Bridge had been blown up. But the 30 Corps met unexpected German resistance, and their assault up Highway 69 halted almost as soon as it began. The Americans were shocked by the lack of urgency among the British armored corps. One officer described that they "stopped for tea." As fellow paratroopers, they knew the British 1st Airborne at Arnhem was not equipped to hold out for long in a defensive mode.

Although it would be the largest parachute drop ever undertaken, they were dropped twelve kilometers from the bridge heads which were the original drop targets. As a result of this error, they were met by two SS divisions, one of which was the Deadly Tiger tanks, the worst that Germany had on the ground.

These "Red Devils," consisting of 320 gliders and 2,300 troops, were dropped eight miles from their target of Arnhem. Half stayed behind to defend the drop zone that night. The landings had alerted German forces, who mobilized the 9th Panzers. They found no one yet at the bridge, so crossed it and took up defensive positions on the road to its south. Only Battalion 2 of the 1st Airborne drop, led by a Scottish Colonel, John Frost, made it to Arnhem that day. Because of the German units on the south side, they could only secure the north bank. They knew they had to hang on for three or four days until 30 Corps could reach them and take over. Due to near total failure of the 1st Airborne's communications, they would be cut off from command most of their time there.

Everything that could possibly go wrong went wrong. The reinforcements that were promised never came. It was a total debacle. Without food or water, and without radio communication, this only added to the disaster. The armor proved to be too light to fight those heavy tanks. It was pretty hopeless.

However, during this paratrooper drop, many farmers helped as best they could. They would help not only children, but Jews, young men on the run, and even Allied airplane crews, that had to bail out of planes after being shot down. This, of course, was extremely dangerous work. Literally hundreds of people were saved by farmers who helped get many of them to safety in Belgium. The courage of the people who were instrumental in doing this was truly unbelievable.

In retrospect, had the plan succeeded, the war's end would not have divided Europe for decennia, in communist and capitalist sections, as was the case in East and West Germany.

Day 2, Monday, September 18: More troops and supplies landed. The US 101st Airborne dealt with the blown bridge at Son by having reconnaissance (advance) units from 30 Corps bringing forward a Bailey bridge to replace it. These amazing bridges were the invention of British Engineer Donald Bailey. A prefabricated truss bridge was designed to be shipped in parts small enough to fit in trucks and be handled by just a few men, and assembled rapidly with no cranes or heavy equipment, but strong enough to support tanks. An astonishing feature was the ability to launch it from one side of the gap, and adjust dimensions to the needs of the site. This is one of the greatest examples of military engineering, credited with making a huge contribution toward ending World War II. This type of bridge is still widely produced and used today.

In Arnhem, while the paratroopers were battling to hold the north side of the road bridge, Scottish Border Regiments were at the original drop zones, securing the area for the next wave of incoming paratroops. The Germans were attacking fiercely, and over-ran the Polish drop zone L, capturing their supplies. At the end of the day, the operation was thirty-six hours behind schedule.

Day 3, Tuesday, September 19: Other ground troops could not break through, but Frost's 2nd Battalion and attached units (600 men) were still in firm control of the northern approach ramp to Arnhem Bridge. Despite heavy shelling by the Germans, which systematically demolished each house to dislodge the defenders, the British clung fiercely to their positions.

Polish Parachutists were delayed in England due to dense fog. Gliders made it through to deliver anti-tank guns and vehicles, but the RAF, not forewarned due to the radio blackout, dropped the supplies over a German-occupied zone.

The US 82nd Airborne was joined by 30 Corps in Nijmegen. Their combined efforts to take the bridge failed. The US 101st with British tanks beat back Panzers at Son and secured the new Bailey bridge.

Day 4, Wednesday, September 20: This was a momentous day in ways both good and bad. First the good news: at Nijmegen, located on the wide Waal River, an arm of the Rhine, boats ordered by the 82nd the day before finally arrived in the afternoon. The Americans lacked training on the British canvas boats, and a shortage of paddles required some to paddle with rifle butts. About half of the twenty-six boats survived the crossing under heavy fire. Survivors assaulted across 200 yards of open ground on the far bank and seized the north end of the bridge, after which German forces withdrew from both ends. After four days of struggle and heavy losses, the Allies had captured one of the two bridges essential to Market-Garden's success!

And the bad news: at the other bridge essential to Market-Garden's success—Arnhem—Frost's forces had been counting on 30 Corps to have arrived by then, but upon finding a way to contact division headquarters mid-day, were told there was no hope of relief from either 30 Corps or more 1st Airborne battalions. By nightfall, they had to cope with 150 wounded lying in the cellars, as food, water, ammunition and medical supplies were running out. They were in and around burning buildings ready to collapse. Under these conditions, a two-hour truce was arranged to evacuate the wounded to German care and captivity, including Frost, who was replaced by Frederick Gough.

The remaining British troops fought bravely, if only with knives. By dawn, German armor had crossed the bridge and had taken the remaining few as prisoners. They radioed a final message, "Out of ammo; God save the king."

They had nothing to be ashamed of. The plan had been for the 10,000-strong 1st Airborne Division to hold Arnhem Bridge for four days. In fact, just 740 men—primarily companies of the 2nd and 4th Battalions—had held it almost as long, against far heavier opposition than anticipated. No wonder that in memory of the fighting there, the bridge rebuilt after the war was renamed John Frost Bridge after Captain John Frost, who fought so gallantly. The people of Arnhem and Oosterbeek did a tremendous job aiding the wounded, as well as serving as informants.

Day 5, Thursday, September 21: To the west of Arnhem Bridge, approximately 3,600 survivors of the 1st Airborne's other battalions were on the outskirts of Oosterbeek. The Germans attacked the perimeter, shrinking the stretch of river held by the British to less than 750 yards, but the paratroopers held on.

After two days of weather delays, the Polish Parachute Brigade was dropped on the south bank. Unfortunately their supplies were dropped far away, and with a missing ferry they had no way to cross the river to Oosterbeek, and so spent the night in Driel. The British found a reliable radio link to 30 Corps artillery support, only to once again learn there was no encouraging news.

Day 6, Friday, September 22: In Oosterbeek, the Germans sought to replicate tactics that had worked well at the Arnhem Bridge, targeting specific positions and even individual houses. They outnumbered survivors of the 1st Airborne four to one. But the Poles at Driel forced the Germans to alter strategy, withdrawing 2,400 troops from Oosterbeek. Finally that morning, three days late, a reconnaissance unit of 30 Corps slipped through fog around Nijmegen and linked up with the Poles at Driel.

That night an unsuccessful attempt was made to boat some of the Poles across the river, using small boats linked by signal cable. The cable consistently broke, forcing the Polish troops to slowly row across against the strong current under enemy observation and fire. With heavy losses, the crossing was halted at dawn.

After multiple skirmishes on Highway 69, the Germans managed to cut the highway and prevent any further advance on Arnhem at this time.

Day 7, Saturday, September 23: The Germans took lessons from the previous day and tried to cut off the British from the river side. The British managed to hold on. Both sides suffered heavy losses. Germans also attacked the Poles on the south side, but were beaten off when tanks from 30 Corps arrived. Boats and engineers from the Canadian army arrived that day. A night-time river crossing landed another 150 Polish troops, but conditions were chaotic and most were captured. The English succeeded in dropping more supplies, but most fell into German hands. A unit of 30 Corps re-took Highway 69.

Day 8, Sunday, September 24: To reinforce the 1ˢᵗ Airborne, two companies of the 4ᵗʰ Battalion—Dorsets—were put across the river. The location was chosen against the advice of Polish General Sosabowski, and the Dorsets landed among prepared German positions. Only seventy-five of the 315 who crossed made it to Oosterbeek; the rest were taken prisoner. A German force re-took Highway 69 between Nijmegen and Arnhem. It was becoming clear that what remained of the great 1ˢᵗ Airborne Division would have to be withdrawn.

Day 9, Monday, September 25: At dawn the British 1ˢᵗ Airborne received orders to retreat across the Rhine that night. During the day, a German assault put the division in some peril, but was finally repulsed. While trying to give the Germans the impression that their positions were unchanged, the 1ˢᵗ Airborne began being ferried across the Rhine on that windy, rainy night. By morning they had withdrawn 2,400 survivors. Over three-hundred men were left to the last, those able to swim across if needed. They were forced to surrender when German fire caught them at first light.

The defense of the "Oosterbeek cauldron" had finally ended. Operation Market-Garden was over, ultimately a failure. Not only had they failed to achieve the ultimate objective, invading Germany, but the 1ˢᵗ Airborne Army was virtually destroyed. Of the 10,000-strong division, just over 2,000 men escaped to Driel. The rest had either been killed or captured. The Germans achieved their victory at a high price, with casualties estimated at 4,000-8,000 of the original 20,000 combatants.

To the south, the newly arrived Northumbrian Division took back the highway from the Germans. The Nijmegen Salient, as it came to be known, was controlled by the Allies after Market-Garden—a corridor from the Belgian border to the area between Nijmegen and Arnhem.

CHAPTER 19

The Hunger Winter

The winter of 1944-45 is forever etched in my mind—and the memories of all Dutch that lived through it. It is known as "the Hunger Winter." As the Netherlands became one of the main western battlefields of the war, a number of factors combined to starve the Dutch people.

First and foremost, we were victims of the widespread dislocation and destruction of war. The retreating German army destroyed locks and bridges to flood the country and impede the Allied advance. This ruined much of the agricultural land.

There were also politics to deal with. By the fall of 1944, or perhaps far before that, Seyss-Inquart had absolutely no delusions that the Dutch would join the Germans in an Aryan nation. He was angered by our resistance during the war. The final straw was when the national railways complied with the exiled Dutch government's appeal for a railway strike to further the Allied liberation efforts. He retaliated by putting an embargo on all food and coal transport to the western Netherlands.

By the time the embargo was partially lifted in November of 1944, allowing restricted food transports over water, the unusually early and harsh winter had already set in. The canals froze over and became impassable for barges. Food stocks in the cities in the western Netherlands quickly ran out. By the end of November, an adult ration in cities like Amsterdam dropped to 400 calories a day. That is less than twenty-five percent of today's recommended daily caloric in-take.

Not even our former miserly bit of food was coming in. There was nothing in the stores anymore. With our ration coupons, we could get some watery substance called potato soup at the neighborhood soup kitchen, which was located in the Asscher Diamond building. This stuff was not edible. There was only one thing, some sort of porridge that was worth standing in line for—and stand in line I did. When we couldn't get that anymore, we made porridge from the grain we collected during our summer in the country. We ground the grain in our coffee mill, and cooked it in water with sweetener. It was awful, and I chose to go to school hungry rather than to eat it.

"Ersatz" was a term used to describe war food at the time— for example, potato peel soup, sugar beet pulp, and anything else undesirable we could scrounge up. Even today, an English dictionary defines "ersatz" to mean a poor imitation or inferior substitute for the real thing. How true! To stretch our meals and add a little bulk, my mother cooked some typical Dutch one pot meals ("stamppot") where you traditionally cook carrots or cabbage and potatoes together, and then she mashed in tulip bulbs.

Because of the danger and widespread hunger in the Netherlands, 200 children, one of my cousins among them, were transported by cattle car over the Afsluit dijk (Closing dike) to farms in Friesland. When he was fifteen, my future husband was sent to the country, where he stayed with a baker, who worked the tar out of the boy. These 200 children were not from all of Amsterdam, but rather were 200 children from a small town annexed to Amsterdam. Some farmers not only helped by sheltering children, but also helped young men who had bailed out of airplanes that were shot down, taking a terrific chance. Many were caught.

By winter of 1945, even the plain stove was useless, as there was no electricity, gas, or coal. Only water and sewer services continued. Someone had the ingenious idea to make an emergency stove. It was more like a three-pound coffee can with a hole cut in the front bottom, in which we could poke small pieces of wood to heat things and do a bit of cooking. Amazing as it may seem, it would heat things. It was so bad that just before the schools closed, my little four-year-old brother came home with a green twig he had found and proudly offered it to my mother for our "stove." How sweet of him, though she knew

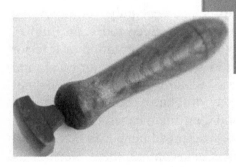

**Top left: The milk cooker.
Top right: The hollow book.
Bottom left: The wax tool my dad used when he cobbled our shoes.**

Bottom: The cast of the operetta group, we played something about gypsies, noticebly by the costumes. Edith played a boy, she is in the second row, fifth from the left. They dressed her with shirt, tie, and a wig. My mother and Mrs. Peters are in the top row.

that green wood does not burn. Of course she pretended she was very happy to have it, and so he did his part!

For light at night, we had a homemade oil lamp—a fancy name for the deep lid of a can filled with a bit of oil and a wick in the middle. It sat on the table and we all clustered around it trying to entertain ourselves. I managed to read and embroider. It was hard; there was no heat and my fingers were very cold. It is the cold I remember more than anything. My father brought home navy blue German sailor sweaters. I needed a dress and I remember cutting one in half, inserting a piece of black velvet my mother had into the waist, to make it a proper dress length. It worked; I embroidered the velvet with various cross stitches by the light of that simple oil lamp. It turned out to be very nice, though not a combination I would use today. It was warm, too!

My dad had made one of our bikes stationary, and one of us would pedal, thus generating a little light from the bicycle lamp. How ingenious people get when the need arises. It was unbelievably cold that winter, with no heat anywhere in the house. Coal was mined in the south, and was impossible to get where we lived in the north.

My father bought twelve hectoliters of coal on the black market; it was in large burlap bags, and he had hoped that at least we could stay warm. I do not know how much it set him back, but unfortunately he had been scammed. The "coal" had been burned before, just cinders, is what they were with a very thin layer of coal on top. My mother was furious, not that my father could help it, but she thought he should have been more observant. School was only sporadically in session now too, as there was no heat there either. As all of the Jewish citizens had been deported or had fled, there were a lot of empty houses in my home town. People broke in and removed anything that would burn, such as doors, floors, window sills, and so on. People were so weakened and frequently very careless; they created cave-ins, fell, and got injured or worse. My father and I talked about that after the war. He never participated in those things.

My Grandfather Otto, before he became employed by the government, was a furniture maker. I still have a beautifully

inlaid box he made. He had made a set of six burgundy uphol-
stered chairs, beautifully carved. I will not forget them, for it
was my task to chop them up for firewood. They would have
been worth a fortune today.

My sister was always a tomboy, with strength and endurance
I never possessed. To this day I envy that trait in her. Yet, we
all have our own strengths in some way. She was twelve when
mom sent her out of town on her bike, to see if she could trade
some large red handkerchiefs and brushes at farms close to
town—and by golly, she came back with milk! Pretty good for a
twelve-year-old girl! We all did our part—I chopped chairs, and
she got milk. We endured unbelievable hardships.

A close call came when my mother was traveling out of town
with a friend, on a bicycle, without tires, of course; the only mode
of transportation left. My father could not go for fear that he
could be picked up and sent to Germany for slave labor. She had
taken some sheets to trade with farmers for food, and was halted
at the town's re-entry port. She was walking, and transporting a
hectoliter of potatoes draped over the bike. Food transport was
absolutely forbidden. The Germans would rather have seen us
starve. I do not know how she managed, but she got to keep the
potatoes. It was during the hunger winter, and even the most hard-
ened soldier could see that the Dutch population was starving.

In January of 1945, we experienced another accidental bomb
drop, which destroyed a large section of the Groenburgwal, and
again cost some victims. We weren't just freezing and starving. The
degradation of the human spirit kept on. In a camp near Amersfoort,
the inmates were forced to sing German songs. In the Jan Luikens
Straat, close to the Concertgebouw (the concert hall), a number of
people were executed. It was another at random execution, which
was a constant thread; we never knew who would get it next.

The Germans still performed their war crimes against
humanity. They were meticulous record-keepers, which really
did not serve them well after the war, because all their atrocities
were recorded by themselves. We had not heard from "Uncle
Max," who was still, as far as we knew, in the Vught concentration camp; the uncertainty must have killed Aunt Mary.

As the winter went on, death from starvation became increasingly common. We knew people would walk hundreds of kilometers to trade valuables for food. The situation in my home town was critical. I recall my Aunt Jeanne going to the park cutting grass and eating it. I saw two women fight for whatever they could steal from each other, a crust of bread as far as I could tell. A totally emaciated woman fell down and died across the street from us.

My brother-in-law once told me he will never forget the sight of carts loaded with bloated bodies, being dumped for burial on the western outskirts of Amsterdam where he lived. I never saw that. In Amsterdam alone, over 18,000 people died of hunger. By one estimate, from September 1944 to the liberation in May of 1945, approximately 30,000 Dutch people starved to death, not to mention the thousands that had become so weakened that they never regained good health.

Shortly before the liberation, some relief came from Sweden—the so-called "Swedish Bread," which was baked in the Netherlands from flour shipped from Sweden. I also recall blue-band margarine and cans of evaporated milk. Soon after that, the German occupiers allowed coordinated air food drops by the Royal Air Force over German-occupied Dutch territory, called Operation Manna. We heard about these food drops, and I wanted to see for myself, but could not get onto our roof, which had a steep pitch. However, at my friend Annie's house there was a flat roof, so up on the roof we went. What a sight it was! I could see the pilots' faces, they flew that low. I waved so hard I thought my arms were going to fall off.

In the last week of the war, the only food we had left was approximately three pounds of potatoes, with no hope of any more after that. Our ration coupons gave us a half loaf of bread per person per week, which was just an ugly looking gray substance, and even that was no longer available, ugly as it was, not even on our ration coupons. In spite of my parents' amazing efforts to feed and clothe us those past five years, there simply was no more to be had.

Fortunately, at this time the war's end truly was at hand, or more of us would have starved to death. By 1944, our beautifully ornate stove was housed in the attic; my father, a very strong man, had carried it upstairs. Now, in its place sat a plain stove with a large flat part, which my mother used to cook things on, that is as long as there were things to cook. She made some sort of syrup from sugar beets, as well as sugar beet cookies. Two weeks before war's end mom paid 45 gulden which would be the same as $45—a fortune—for a loaf of bread. From what substance it was made I do not know, but when she sliced into it maggots came crawling out. She was outraged when we discovered this precious food was disgusting and inedible.

During the Hunger Winter, neither trams nor trains were running anymore, and in this exceptionally cold winter, we had to take drastic measures to keep warm, or people would have frozen to death. On occasion, my father, Uncle Dirk, and my ten-year-old brother Freddy would go to the train tracks to get out some of the biels (railroad ties). It was Fred's task to pry loose the little blocks holding the ties in place. They would steal railroad ties and bring them home for firewood. They were shot at, but thank goodness not hit or hurt.

I accompanied Annie to church one Sunday morning, and on the walk home, we almost got shot. In back of us was a large square; close to us, a bridge across the river Amstel, from which Amsterdam derives its name. There were streets on both sides along the river, as well as between the square and the bridge. In the middle were the tracks of the tram, which was no longer running; in fact nothing was running any more that last year of the war.

On the bridge was a man on a tireless bicycle. Any rubber tires had to be brought in, for the Germans needed the material for the war. Suddenly there was a lot of shouting, and the German voices screamed, "Halt!" We did not know if it was us they were commanding, so we stopped, just waiting for a moment to see if they had meant us; but no. Seconds later, bullets were flying past our heads. Thank God they flew over our heads. We ran for cover onto the side street, and stayed hidden, crouched in a doorway until the shooting stopped and the assault squad had left. The young man with the bike lay dead on the bridge; yet another victim of this senseless war.

We were more fortunate than many. We did have some food, on occasion. My mother added anything that was edible to provide us food. She added tulip bulbs and sugar beets to potatoes. We had no meat during the entire winter. My aunt would go to the park and get grass to eat.

This war became my father's small, personal battle, in contrast to the terrible one on a huge scale. The Allied raids into Germany's Ruhr industrial complexes from March to July 1943, involved roughly eight hundred aircraft flying 18,000 individual missions, passing overhead. We could hear the droning of many aircraft, and once again saw the search lights crisscrossing the night sky as well as hearing the sounds of the German gun batteries trying to shoot down as many aircraft as possible, right over our heads.

A four-night raid on Hamburg in July had provoked a firestorm that literally burned the town to cinders, covering roughly 62,000 acres. A firestorm is not an effect that a bombing force can achieve at will. It requires the perfect combination of weather conditions, coupled with failure of civil defense systems. The central conflagration feeds on oxygen drawn from the periphery by winds which can reach cyclone speed, suffocating the people in cellars and bunkers, and raising temperatures so high that every flammable thing burns by spontaneous combustion. Such were the conditions in Hamburg the week of July 24, 1943. It had been a period of hot, dry weather. The initial bombardment had broken the water mains in hundreds of places, and the fire's temperature at the core reached 1,500 degrees Fahrenheit. Eighty percent of Hamburg's buildings were destroyed by the firestorm, and 30,000 of its inhabitants were killed. Just imagine—30,000 dead.

I hate to think of it now, but we were actually happy when we heard the drone of hundreds of Allied airplanes overhead, thinking of them on their way to bomb German towns. The fire storm of Hamburg was something we neither knew, nor cared about, at the time. The hope of the Allied pilots was to get through to England or the Northern part of France where the English Channel is at its narrowest. Their first goal was for safety; the second was to continue fighting.

The Allies could have taken Germany with greater speed had they been able to cross the Rhine river. Of the 10,000 Brits, only 2,300 remained of which 1,800 were taken prisoner. Only 500 escaped with the help of the Dutch population and the Dutch resistance.

We knew only that there were constant air battles going on. Of course, the Germans didn't want the bombs to fall on their towns; they tried to get as many Allied planes out of their air as possible to over our country. You could actually see them being shot down. It was very dangerous. We didn't know where the planes would fall if they came down; most were burning, and the pilots had no choice in the matter; when their engines failed they tried to spare homes below if at all possible.

We did not know what or where the targets were, but we knew it was somewhere in Germany, and that the outcome would eventually bring the Germans to their knees. I later learned the details. A specially trained squadron #617 had destroyed the Mohne and Eder Dams which supplied the Ruhr Valley with much of its hydroelectricity. In August, a major raid destroyed the laboratories and workshops at Peenemunde, where pilot-less missiles were being built.

My mother understood the danger. My sister and I had a room in the attic. When the planes entered the coastline, the air raid sirens would wail, and mom would always come get us out of our beds, and require us to sit on her bed. It was really silly, because if a bomb or a plane had fallen on our house, we'd all be dead. So I begged my mother to please let me stay in my own bed, and just let me sleep, because I'd be so tired the next morning. But it was her idea that somehow we would be safer if she could just keep us near. I don't blame her now. Indeed, having become a parent myself later, and looking back, I truly can relate to her fears and her need to do something to combat them.

CHAPTER 20

Wasted Wisdom

What if the Allies—England in particular—had trusted and turned to what Dutch military leaders and the underground resistance had to offer? Historians see much to indicate it would have ended the war in 1944 and spared us the horrors of the final winter of the war.

The stage for Market-Garden's failure was set by an earlier incident, "The Great Mistake," which ignored what the Belgian Resistance had to offer. It occurred at the Scheldt estuary, where the river, which flowed north through Belgium, turns west to the North Sea in Zeeland, the Netherlands' most southwest province. As mentioned earlier, the significance of the Scheldt for both commerce and war is that it connects Antwerp to the North Sea, allowing it to be the major world port it has been for centuries.

At this point in the war, Antwerp was recognized as critical to bringing Allied supplies ashore closer to the fighting front, easing logistical burdens in their supply lines that stretched hundreds of miles from Normandy eastward to the Siegfried Line in Germany. As September 1944 arrived, various Allied forces had liberated France; British troops pushed into Belgium, capturing Brussels on September 3 and Antwerp on September 4. The ultimate goal was to push on through the Netherlands and into Germany. But the advance halted with the British in possession of Antwerp while the Germans still controlled the Scheldt estuary which gave it access to the North Sea. Allied shipping to the port was therefore still impossible.

When the British 11th Armored Division rolled into Antwerp on September 4, they met no resistance. With Belgian assistance they quickly captured the vital docks and related port facilities. But they failed to seize bridges over the western end of the Albert Canal that ran through the area. The Belgian Resistance implored whoever would hear them to send whatever forces they could muster to seize a crossing over the Canal at Merxem, send an armored column with all possible speed to the Beveland peninsula, quickly reinforce the column, and seal off the peninsula where it joined the mainland.

The battered German 15th Army, under the command of General von Zangen, had been holding the southern bank of the Scheldt Estuary, ordered to reinforce the Channel ports. At the risk of being trapped with their backs to the North Sea, as the Canadian First Army advanced on them from the south. They were ordered to evacuate across the waters of the Scheldt to the German-held island of Walcheren, march eastward along the connecting road to the Beveland Peninsula, and hence to the Dutch mainland north of Antwerp. The Resistance recognized a unique opportunity to catch the resilient German forces off guard, bottling them up in the Beveland peninsula and stopping them from controlling mainland access to the vital port of Antwerp. The Great Mistake was losing this fleeting opportunity.

No one in the chain of command, four commanders who were normally alert to tactical opportunities—Montgomery (21st Army Group) to Dempsey (2nd Army) to Horrocks (30 Corps) to Roberts (11th Armored Division)—thought of issuing orders to control the bridges and capture this strategic peninsula. Apparently, given Eisenhower's broad directive to "undertake operations aimed at the heart of Germany," somewhere in the rush across France no one was paying enough attention to intermediate objectives such as opening the port of Antwerp.

It didn't help that reports from British Intelligence to the senior commanders at the end of August were incomplete and inaccurate. We do know the commanders would have made better-informed decisions if they had been briefed about the effective Belgian Resistance, which could have provided expert and accurate knowledge of local conditions.

In addition, in early 1944, an exiled Belgian had helped prepare for the British a handbook about critical infrastructure in Belgium. This handbook had already identified problems and presented solutions, but they were not communicated to any of the involved Allied commanders who could have used it to very great advantage.

Had the British seized the opportunity immediately, historians agree they would have succeeded against very light and disorganized opposition, effectively eliminating the German 15th Army and avoiding the need for the bloody Battle of the Scheldt in October and November, which finally opened the sea route to Antwerp. Would it have made a difference to open that port in early September? Think about this: On October 1, over 240 Allied supply ships were waiting in the North Sea, unable to unload their cargo because of the limited port facilities on the continent, and unable to use Antwerp. It sure seems to me that this would have made a difference in speeding up the ending of the war.

By September 6, it was known that the Great Mistake had allowed 86,000 men and 600 artillery pieces of the 15th Army to connect up with the Replacement Army under new Commander-in-Chief West Gerd von Rundstedt. Thus reinforced, he stabilized the western front, and coordinated the German defense against the expected massive Allied attack. Ultimately von Zangen's 15th Army helped defeat the Allies in Operation Market-Garden, which prolonged the war for us by eight months. Yes, it was a "Great Mistake" to fail to stop them at the Scheldt.

I have described the massive military operation from historical writings. Yet, what if the Dutch military and Resistance had been allowed to make a difference in Operation Market-Garden? How might history have been changed?

On September 3, Queen Wilhelmina had announced that Prince Bernhard was in command of both the Dutch military and the underground. On September 6, the date we learned of the Great Mistake at Antwerp, Dutch Royalty re-entered the Western Front. Prince Bernhard arrived in France that evening to pay his respects to British Field Marshal Montgomery. Our prince was an accomplished pilot who flew the plane himself, accompanied by two fighter planes. He came with a small staff and a briefcase stuffed to the hilt with Dutch resistance reports. On September 7, he and his staff set out for Belgium.

At Laeken he was met by General Horrocks, commander of 30 Corps, and was ushered in to meet Montgomery, who was not happy to see him. Montgomery had a lot on his mind, and the presence of royalty in his area he could do without. Or so he thought.

The thirty-three-year-old prince was the same age as my father at the time. The prince was in awe of Montgomery, but the man's demeanor made it difficult for Bernhard to converse easily with him, unlike General Eisenhower's easy-going attitude.

Blunt and to the point, Montgomery told the prince it would be unwise to visit the Irene Brigade, the Dutch unit attached to the British 2nd Army, quartered in Diest, about ten miles from the front line in Belgium. Our prince, as commander in chief of the Dutch forces, had every intention of visiting Diest, but for the moment let it go. Instead, he began to discuss the Dutch resistance reports. However, Montgomery interrupted him, reiterating that he would not allow the prince to stay in Diest.

Irked, Bernhard felt compelled to point out that he was serving directly under Eisenhower, and did not come under the field marshal's command. This comment did not earn him favor with Montgomery, who was reported to be Eisenhower's bitter opponent when it came to war strategies, although Eisenhower later agreed with Montgomery about keeping the Prince out of Diest, basing him in liberated Brussels instead.

At this time Montgomery did grudgingly inform the Prince that there were plans for a large airborne drop in the very near future. Bernhard went on to review the reports of the Dutch underground. Montgomery was told of the makeup of the resistance groups, but bluntly told the Prince, "I don't think your resistance can be of much use to us, therefore I believe all of this to be quite unnecessary."

In the years since the war, there is a theory about this. It had been discovered in April 1944 that Britain's spy network in the

Netherlands had been thoroughly and famously compromised—the so-called "England Game." Some said the British minimized all civilian contact in Market-Garden because they assumed the Dutch Resistance was similarly penetrated. But Bernhard knew the people who were running the underground groups, and how the information was one hundred percent correct. Indeed, it is now generally accepted that the Dutch Resistance in that war was the best organized in Europe. Nonetheless, the detailed information in Bernhard's possession from the Dutch underground was discounted or ignored.

The ultimate goal of Operation Market-Garden was to take the bridge at the village of Arnhem. The underground had a cell structure, and each cell was called a fight group, "knokploeg" or KP. The Arnhem KP was known as one of the finest in the country, with both trained combat members and well-educated technical personnel. These men and women had set up a network of secret telephone lines to the already liberated south and to other KP members throughout the country, unknown to the enemy and safe for the Resistance to use.

In the days leading up to Operation Market-Garden, the Arnhem KP had reported to England an increasing amount of German movement in the area, with accurate identification of armor units and their commanders. Staff cars of high-ranking SS officers had been spotted. As we know today, these reports were backed by British intelligence as they monitored German radio traffic and by photos from an aerial reconnaissance flight showing tanks deployed only fifteen miles from the proposed drop zones. There were also reports of an SS training school near the tanks.

Montgomery argued the tanks must be there because they were broken down and inoperable. He was in denial, unwilling or unable to make changes to the plans. Apparently no one in authority was prepared to accept that German forces were of sufficient strength to trouble the mighty 1st Airborne. The reality was that the Panzer regiment refitting in Arnhem did mean trouble. They were combat-ready German reinforcements, with specific training in anti-airborne assault tactics, roughly 3,000-strong, right at the drop zones. Five hours after the first landing, Panzers had crossed the Arnhem Bridge, with no British troops yet in sight, and had moved on to defend the approach from Nijmegen.

If only the Britons had heeded the advance intelligence. Instead, they continued to make plans, albeit hastily, all done in about a week. Also, senior Dutch military advisors were excluded from the planning. At first, because of Montgomery's vast experience, Bernhard and his staff did not question this. It never entered their minds that costly mistakes could be made at the top. They resigned themselves to just hope and wait.

However, had they known in advance about the choice of drop zones, and the distance between them and the Arnhem bridge, the prince and his staff certainly could have said something. Because it wasn't just an issue of the sixty-mile distance that 30 Corps must travel to relieve the paratroops at Arnhem Bridge. It was the nature of the road corridor to get there.

Highway 69 became known as Hell's Highway, described as a "battlefront two tanks wide," running dike-like through marshy terrain called "polder," low land reclaimed from the sea. From the moment Dutch generals learned of the route that Horrocks' columns proposed to take, they tried to dissuade anyone who would listen. They warned of the dangers of using the narrow, exposed roads, with no ability to take tanks off the roadway, or bring in supplies from the sides.

General Doorman described how he had personally held trials with armored vehicles before the war in precisely that area, and warned Montgomery's staff that the tightly-scheduled three-day advance would be unlikely, if not impossible, unless infantry accompanied the tanks. Vehicles moving on this long narrow road would be easy targets for air and ground attacks.

Everyone in the British camp was exceptionally polite, but the warnings fell on deaf ears. The Brits preferred to do their own thing. The general impression amongst Dutch staff was that the British considered them a bunch of idiots for daring to question their military tactics.

As the operation was put into play, things went from bad to worse. From his post in Brussels, Prince Bernhard followed each harrowing new development with anguish. By day five of what was supposed to have been no more than a four-day operation, the prince was informed of a particularly unfortunate error, and lost his temper—something rare for him. He angrily demanded to know of his chief of staff, why wouldn't the British listen to them? From his Brussels headquarters, Bernhard had kept our queen and the Dutch government, in exile in London, fully informed of the events. But they could not have influenced British military decisions, either. Churchill would never have interfered.

Queen Wilhelmina followed the battle anxiously. Like Bernhard, she had expected—or at least hoped for—a quick liberation of the Netherlands. But the royal family knew if Market-Garden failed what cruelty and reprisals the Germans would bestow upon our people. As told by Cornelius Ryan in his book, *A Bridge Too Far*, the queen hated the Germans with a passion. When informed by Prince Bernhard that some of the royal castles and estates would soon be overrun, she replied, "Burn them all. I will never again set foot in a place where the Germans have been sitting in my chair, in my room. Never!" Bernhard argued that they were useful buildings. "We can steam them out, use DDT." The queen still insisted, "Burn the palaces down." When Bernhard refused, and even went so far as to occupy one with his staff, she did not talk to him for weeks, except on official matters.

As the operation drew to its unsuccessful close, Bernhard knew that with the exception of a handful of senior officers, he was not particularly loved at Montgomery's headquarters, because what he had said was now turning out to be true. And no one was more aware of the operation's problems than the Dutch Resistance in Arnhem.

Plagued by poor communications planning and near-total failure of British radios, the 1st Airborne would be out of touch with most other headquarters for much of the battle. It didn't need to be that way, but again, the Brits wouldn't listen or accept what the Dutch Resistance had to offer.

Before they took off from England, all 1st Airborne troops received instructions to ignore the Dutch Resistance because they were poorly organized and/or infiltrated by the enemy. Despite these orders, it is known that one line between a safe house near the bridge and a safe house at Oosterbeek was kept open. The commander of Arnhem KP made contact several times with the British 1st Airborne headquarters at Oosterbeek, offering information about German activities, such as when a new group of tanks was heading in their direction, and trying to convince them to use the underground's secure communication system. The reply? "Everything is under control. We don't need your assistance."

Not everyone distrusted the Resistance. A few days before Operation Market-Garden was launched, several SAS men were dropped in the region with the mission of connecting to underground groups and helping them to organize as a fighting force. The recruited Dutch volunteers proved ready to support the airborne troops once they had landed. These included a party of twenty-five Dutch commandos who had seen action in the Far East against the Japanese, and now home, returned to action, assigned within all four airborne divisions.

The Germans had blocked the Dutch people from using the public telephone lines for anything except emergency calls, which included fire, medical, and police. However, they themselves made full use of the public exchange. Knowing this, Dutch telephone operators tried to sabotage German communications, and were successful for a time. This significantly delayed German operations during the first hours of the Arnhem battle, when they were forced to use couriers on bikes to get orders to their units.

Dutch operators also tapped the German lines. When they intercepted messages about preparations to blow up the bridge, the information was immediately passed on to Frost's headquarters, and a platoon was able to remove the explosives.

Although very frustrated that the important information they could provide was being ignored, Arnhem KP kept trying to help. They used their secret lines to contact Allied headquarters and request an air strike to stop the advanced Panzer group on the road from Dieren to Arnhem, but the call was cut off and the request ignored. At least the U.S. Airborne Divisions, lacking the skepticism of the British, made active use of Dutch Resistance members as guides and sources of intelligence.

How ironic that the commander of the Dutch Resistance, Prince Bernhard, based one hundred miles from Arnhem, knew exactly what was happening in his country because of detailed reports he received from Arnhem KP, but General Urquhart, commander of the forces in Arnhem and Oosterbeek, had to guess what was happening with his forces.

Even when most disenchanted with Montgomery and his staff, the prince blamed no one in the field. American and British soldiers were giving their lives to rid the Netherlands of a cruel oppressor.

I believe the saddest "what if" I learned is that simple knowledge of the alternative crossings to Arnhem Bridge could have changed the outcome of the operation. Driel Ferry could have been easily secured by Frost's paratroops. Or just fifteen miles west was a bridge similar to Arnhem— the Thenen—which was undefended due to all efforts being directed on Oosterbeek. 30 Corps could have crossed unopposed into the rear of the German lines.

In all of Operation Market-Garden, 35,000 Allied troops participated, with 17,000 casualties. Of the 10,000 men of the British 1st Airborne dropped into Arnhem, 1,500 died and over 6,000 were prisoners of war. Twenty-five hundred of those survived, five hundred by escaping with the help of the Dutch Resistance in the Pegasus operations.

To get the hidden men out of our country was an extremely dangerous mission. The people helping with this knew that at any moment they could lose their freedom; more likely, they would be shot immediately.

The most readable history of Operation Market-Garden, in my opinion, remains Ryan's book, *A Bridge Too Far.* In 1977, the book was adapted to a star-studded film of the same name, directed by Richard Attenborough. It did a fair job of presenting the human drama, including the death and destruction suffered by Dutch civilians; not only the soldiers lost their lives. Many civilians became victims of brutalities and were shot without reason. During the 1990s, I went to the cemetery where these fallen men are buried. The endless rows of crosses brought tears to my eyes; it still does.

The Dutch Resistance lost many workers, but never stopped its work. An estimated 9,000 active Resistance members were killed in fighting, captured and executed, or died in concentration camps. Another 9,000 are estimated to have fled the Netherlands during the occupation, and perished while serving as secret agents or as soldiers with Allied forces.

September 26, the day after the battle ended and Allied soldiers had withdrawn, orders were given for the evacuation of the area. About 100,000 people had to leave their homes and seek shelter elsewhere. These were the locals who had done so much to share information, treat the wounded, and aid the escape of those left behind. Arnhem and Oosterbeek became ghost towns. When the people returned, many found their houses destroyed and looted of everything that could be used by the Germans. They had to start all over again.

A memorial to the people of Arnhem's province, Gelderland, reads: "Fifty years ago, British and Polish Airborne soldiers fought here against overwhelming odds to open the way into Germany and bring the war to an early end. Instead we brought death and destruction for which you have never blamed us. This stone marks our admiration for your great courage, remembering especially the women who tended our wounded. In the long winter that followed, your families risked death by hiding Allied soldiers and airmen, while members of the Resistance led many to safety."

Montgomery wrote in his memoirs, "In my prejudiced view, if the operation had been properly backed from its inception, and given the aircraft, ground forces and administrative resources necessary for the job, it would have succeeded in spite of my mistakes, or the adverse weather, or the presence of the SS Panzer Corps in the Arnhem area. I remain Market Garden's unrepentant advocate." At the time he publicly called Market-Garden "ninety percent successful."

Prince Bernhard's response to this was made to Cornelius Ryan: "My country can never again afford the luxury of another Montgomery success."

Hans Moederzoon van Kuilenburg

CHAPTER 21

Battles South

The village of Overloon, just north of the larger town of Venray, had for four years escaped the dire consequences of war. However, on September 26, 1944, the war reached the narrow strip of land between Eindhoven and Arnhem that had just been liberated by the Nijmegen Bridge forces during Operation Market Garden and was slowly being extended.

The Germans had established a fortified line on the eastern border of North Brabant, a southern province that is north only in relation to the Belgian border. They hoped to prevent the Allied Forces from crossing the Meuse River at the narrow Limburg peninsula and invading Germany. The German defense, equipped with armored technology, had created a seemingly impregnable line, their manpower estimated at eight times that of the Allies.

Both parties bombarded each other for the first four days. On September 30, the Allies launched an attack with the help of the U.S. 7th Armored Division, which had been specially drafted for that purpose. Thus began the fiercest battle in Western Europe since D-Day, and the first and only tank battle ever to take place in the Netherlands. It pitted American Sherman tanks against German Panzers. The American Sherman tanks tried to breach the German defenses but over and over they were prevented by the German mine fields, field artillery and tanks. This was the start of one of the fiercest battles that took place in Western Europe.

For over a week the Americans failed to breach German lines. On October 8, they were relieved by British armored and infantry divisions. A new assault was to be launched four days later, but the Allied tanks literally bogged down in the soft ground once again. So the difficult task of breaking German resistance was given to the infantry.

First an immense air raid pounded the German positions, and reduced Overloon and Venray to nothing but rubble. British ground troops slowly advanced, fighting over each ruined house or barn. Two days of intense battle ensued before the last German stronghold fell in Overloon.

The Germans, however, redeployed to the forest, where their snipers picked off our advancing soldiers. When their ammunition was gone, the Germans used fixed bayonets, and man-to-man combat raged. But the British advanced, inch by inch.

Heavy fighting continued at the rain-swollen Molenbeek, which the British dubbed Blood Creek after finding it was booby-trapped with mines and strategically covered by German gun emplacements. The Allied capture of the bridge took more than a day, followed by heavier fighting in Venray.

Then a see-saw of counteroffensives began. As soon as the British transferred some of their units to clear the enemy from the western part of Brabant, the Germans reorganized and used their bridgehead on the Meuse River at Venlo to launch a thrust westwards, eventually reaching where the British had established their headquarters. By the time the Allies regrouped to face this attack, only heavy fighting would dislodge the Germans from their new positions and push them back. It was not until November 22 that Venray, or what was left of it, was again liberated by the Allies.

By December 3, German troops were pushed back across the river Meuse at the German border, but not without first inflicting heavy casualties and destruction to the area and its residents. Civilians did not welcome evacuation orders, and my fellow countrymen especially took their sweet time if the orders came from the Germans; an order from Allied forces received much faster action.

But hiding in no-man's land was not a smart thing for civilians. One man hid with a friend in an underground shelter between some haystacks, and barely escaped alive when a German tank crushed it. As the see-saw battle progressed, both men were exposed to the dangers of the crossfire. For days they hid, surviving on apples from shot-up trees. And the ordeal didn't end when they made it back to their home. On October 12 alone, 900,000 grenades landed on Overloon. Understandably, the horrors of war were to stay with them for a lifetime.

Meanwhile, the people living west of the River Meuse, behind the frontline of the corridor, were severely put to the test as well. The German army had trucked in ammunition to the front line, and filled the now empty trucks for the return trip with anything of value "found" in the evacuated homes or farms—or stolen at gun point in plain view of the distraught owners who couldn't do much except grit their teeth. Those who did resist giving up their valuables were shot. Retreating troops often took livestock and horses as well, driving the animals away in the direction of the Meuse.

Civilians risked more than losing their belongings. After many unsuccessful labor conscription efforts by the Germans to dig trenches, they combed the area for men between the ages of sixteen and sixty. Later these orders were accompanied by ever stronger threats of violence against hostages, both men and women. All this and more unnerving situations went on while "friendly fire" from the Allies was killing many civilians.

The battle code-named Operation Aintree was also described by Allied commanders as a "second Caen," referring to the battlegrounds of Normandy in June of 1944. The liberation of this part of the south was achieved at the cost of many lives and much property. Allied losses at Overloon numbered 1,878 men, forty tanks and three airplanes. German losses were 600 men with hundreds of their soldiers taken captive.

Just as the battle of Overloon followed closely on the heels of Market-Garden, so did the return to the mission of opening up the port of Antwerp, which was in British hands, by clearing the Germans from their fortified positions in Scheldt estuary, which connected Antwerp to the sea. In "The Great Mistake" of September 4, 1944, the Allies had wasted a brief moment of opportunity to disable the Germans. For the rest of that month, they had turned their attention to Market-Garden. Now they returned to finish things at the Scheldt, but soon learned the Germans had put the intervening weeks to good use in planning their defense of the estuary.

The Battle of the Scheldt was a five-week offensive beginning October 2, 1944. It consisted of three parts, all conducted over daunting geography. It was fought primarily by the 1st Canadian Army, bolstered by attached troops from several other countries.

Part one was a campaign to clear South Beveland Peninsula, stretching from the mainland to Walcheren Island. It began by fighting north from Antwerp. Canadian forces attacked over open, flooded land, contending with driving rain, booby traps and land mines. This was the only part of the Scheldt battle conducted in Belgium. From there on, they were in the Dutch province of Zeeland.

On October 3, 7, and 11, RAF bombers breached the island's dikes in four places, flooding the central part of the island, unfortunately with severe civilian loss of life. But the flooding forced the Germans to high ground and allowed the use of amphibious vehicles by the Allies. The island was then attacked from three directions—across the causeway from the east, across the Scheldt from the south, and by sea from the west. German resistance was fierce, defending their retreating lines with artillery and snipers. But by November 8, it was finished. Over 41,000 Germans were taken prisoner. Allied casualties were almost 13,000, half of them Canadians.

By October 24, the Allies were ready for Operation Vitality, the advance down the peninsula. Additional Allied forces protected the region from outside attacks and made sure the Canadians wouldn't be cut off on the peninsula. They encountered mines, mud and strong enemy defenses at Beveland Canal, which were finally outflanked by a British amphibious assault. It took several attempts, with heavy casualties, but eventually the Germans were cleared from the peninsula.

While this was going on, Operation Switchback used Canadian and Polish forces to clear the Breskens Pocket, which lay along the southern bank of the West Scheldt arm of the estuary, extending from the northern coast back towards Antwerp. It was a two-pronged assault, with one brigade fighting to cross heavily defended canals, at times using flamethrowers that reached across the canals, with another brigade mounting an amphibious attack from the coastal side of the pocket. Success was achieved, but only after a month of heavy fighting.

The final part of the triangular battle was for Walcheren Island, at the end of the Beveland Peninsula and off the coast of Breskens, the only area that still remained in German hands. It was defended by heavy coastal batteries and was strongly fortified against amphibious assaults. The only land approach was a long narrow road from South Beveland Peninsula, just a raised two-lane road, surrounded by marshy flats.

Once the German defenders were no longer a threat, it took another three weeks to de-mine the harbors. The first ship carrying Allied supplies unloaded in Antwerp on November 29, and convoys started bringing a steady stream of supplies to the continent, sustaining the Allied drive towards Germany. The Germans clearly recognized the importance of this deep-water port to the Allies, because they fired more V-1/V-2 "flying bombs" at Antwerp than other city in the war. The first pilotless guided missiles used in war were the forerunners of today's cruise missiles. The port was never destroyed, but the city itself was severely damaged and rebuilt after the war.

The German desire to retake Antwerp was also a pivotal objective of their last and largest offensive in the west, a bold plot hatched by Hitler and launched on December 15, 1944, which sent German troops storming across Belgium and Luxembourg toward Antwerp.

This was the famed Battle of the Bulge, or Ardennes (Belgium) offensive, the largest and bloodiest of the battles American forces experienced in World War II, fought by some 600,000 Americans and a smaller number of British troops. At first the Germans smashed the Americans, who had ignored warnings and were ill-prepared for the German buildup. By January 30, 1945, the Allies had turned the tide and won the battle, but their losses of troops and equipment set their own offensive timetable back by months. Casualty estimates varied widely, ranging from 70,000 to 100,000 Allies; all but 1,500 were American. German losses are estimated at 60,000 to 100,000.

The impact on Germany was dramatic. Not only had their Army in the West been pushed back, but the tanks and soldiers lost in the Ardennes would not be available for the defense of Germany herself, or to halt the Soviets on the Eastern Front. By early 1945, it could no longer escape the Germans' attention that they had lost the war. The villa owned by my Uncle Harry, which for five years had been full of German nurses and their officer boyfriends, had emptied out, as the nurses went back to Germany. Karel, too, had to move, again.

Our Aunt Carrie, who was close in age to Karel, cousin Nini, his sister, and Karel all traveled from Amersfoort to Amsterdam on their dilapidated bikes, their only mode of transportation. Luckily it was typical Dutch weather—rain and wind—and all three were wearing headscarves and raincoats, all made up, including Karel looking like a girl, or so they hoped. At a gateway at the entrance of town, they were halted by a sentry. Karel had no papers of any kind; so he kept on slowly pedaling. My aunt caused a commotion, speaking fluent German. She started to cry stating they lost their papers, whereupon the sentry let them go. Fooled the Germans? It's likely they were tired of war, too. Sadly, Karel passed away in 2007; Tim died in 2010.

Hitler's gamble shortened the war by months. But it didn't end soon enough to spare us our toughest time in the war. While the military were fighting in the Ardennes, the civilians of occupied Holland were fighting a losing battle against cold and starvation.

CHAPTER 22

Of Peace and Prison Camps

Germany could not succeed in fighting a two-front war, and it was clear an Allied victory was inevitable. On April 30, 1945, the Russians reached Berlin, just before the U.S. arrived. On that same day, Adolph Hitler committed suicide. He was succeeded by Admiral Donitz, who negotiated the surrender of the war, and VE Day, which stood for "Victory in Europe," was celebrated on May 5, 1945.

Throughout Hitler's reign of terror, the SS had remained loyal and accountable to only Hitler. From its inception, the SS had spread fear and destruction throughout Germany and Europe. This finally ended with Hitler's suicide.

Just a month earlier President Roosevelt had died, and was succeeded by Harry Truman. The U.S. military was preparing to invade Japan, although a Japanese defeat appeared inevitable. In an effort to avoid heavy U.S. casualties, Truman approved the dropping of atomic bombs on Japan. On August 6, Hiroshima was bombed, and on August 9, Nagasaki was devastated by a nuclear attack. Japan opened peace negotiations on August 10 and the surrender occurred on August 14, 1945.

The Dutch played a limited role in the Asian theater, but a role nonetheless. On January 10, 1942, the Japanese invaded the Dutch East Indies, now Indonesia. Dutch navy ships there joined the American-British-Dutch-Australian (ABDA) fleet, commanded by Dutch admiral Karel Doorman. On February 27, he was ordered to take the offensive against the Japanese, and the fleet engaged at the Battle of the Java Sea, where the ABDA fleet was destroyed.

After Japanese troops had landed on Java, the Dutch surrendered on March 1, 1942. Dutch submarines escaped and resumed the fight with the Allies, and several Dutch army and navy pilots fought with the Royal Australian Air Force, participating in the eventual liberation of the Netherlands East Indies. The largest Allied invasion took place in July 1945.

Despite the Allied victory, the Dutch were about to lose their sole claim to an overseas "empire." The Japanese had already begun independence negotiations with Indonesian nationalists, and after the surrender of the Japanese, nationalists fought a four-year war which led to Dutch recognition of the independence of Indonesia. There remains to this day a lasting Indonesian influence in Dutch culture and cuisine.

On April 13, 1945, Operation Veritable was launched in the Rhineland, approaching Arnhem from the east instead of the south. This time, after just two days of fighting, the city of Arnhem was finally liberated by the Canadians. It was finally over; suddenly every city block had outdoor parties. What fun that was. I learned to jitterbug with Canadian soldiers. I literally danced the summer of 1945 away.

After our northern provinces were liberated in May of 1945, we learned to our dismay how much the South had suffered from open warfare. Until then, we only knew that our isolation meant no food or coal for heat could reach us. We assumed all was well in the liberated south. We did not know that hundreds of civilians—men, women and children—never lived to see their liberation day. No wonder the locals still refer to it as "The Forgotten Battle," something most Dutch people knew little about until the final liberation.

The property damage was beyond description. Thousands of homes were gone, hundreds of farms leveled, entire city districts flattened, and almost 100 of the 270 historic Roman Catholic churches in the diocese of Roermond damaged beyond repair.

However, some positive things did rise from the devastation. Several northern Dutch municipalities which were spared destruction themselves went on to spearhead fundraising campaigns to help towns in Brabant and Limburg provinces. Both

Venray and Overloon were completely rebuilt. They are "new towns," with not a home in existence built before 1944. Especially heartening is that Venray's church tower, which had been blown up by retreating German troops, was rebuilt with a substantial donation from post-war Germany. Food was still scarce and everything was so depleted.

I walked far out of town to greet our liberators, but was bitterly disappointed when they did not offer me a ride into town on their tanks, like they did the older girls. In retrospect, that was probably best, even though it hurt at the time. Nobody would even look at an undernourished teenager. I saw little kids just wanting to touch the liberators; I remember a seven- or eight-year- old girl just pawing a soldier's face; I think he understood and did not seem to mind. The joy was so great.

On May 7, two days after the war had officially ended, on the Dam Square, and in front of the queen's palace, we were not aware that some of the enemy had holed up in a large store and a church. They opened fire and machine gunned the jubilant Dutch families that were out for an afternoon stroll. Those cowards shot and killed over a hundred men, women, and children, including babies in buggies, in broad daylight.

After the war ended, as in other liberated countries, Dutch citizens began taking the law into their own hands. Groups of men armed with sten guns—"machine guns"—were everywhere, arresting collaborators. This was a good thing, but I questioned the number of men that suddenly sprung up as resistance; they were everywhere. Those that profited by constructing pillboxes, etc., should be punished, as should those who joined the Nazi party and perpetuated its terrors. Some were lynched without a trial; men who had volunteered and fought with the German army or that had belonged to the so hated Waffen-SS were used to clear minefields and rightly suffered great losses. Dutch women who had been known to have had sexual relations with the enemy were arrested and dealt with by the resistance.

My girlfriend and I were on a walk in downtown Amsterdam about two weeks after the war's end, when we spotted a large crowd of people at the Dam Square. On a scaffold in front of the palace stood a young woman, her head shaved. Forced to stand on a scaffold, she was visible to many from quite a distance. She must have been accused of a very serious crime, perhaps spying. I don't know for sure. However, just as we got there, they poured hot tar over her head, and then covered her with chicken feathers. They then paraded her around the square. I had to leave the square as the sight of this woman covered in hot tar was too much for me to handle. The hatred was truly palpable. This sight haunted me for years.

I saw several other women's heads being shaved because they had been involved with someone from the occupying forces, but thank God not tarred and feathered. It was also common to paint their shaved heads orange; I imagine the color had something to do with the surname of the Royal family.

My Uncle Henk only became my uncle in 1952 when he married my father's younger sister. After the war, Uncle Henk had become a bus driver on a bus my Aunt took to work every day. He was a quiet, unassuming man, who never realized he was my hero. He, his sister and her husband, were in one of the first resistance groups that had sprung up almost immediately after the German occupation of the Netherlands. They were members of the CPN, a communist oriented party, which was a regular political party at the time. They were betrayed in 1941. Henk was sent to Buchenwald in Germany. His sister and her husband went to another concentration camp, though I have no knowledge to which camp. Unfortunately neither of them survived.

Uncle Henk was in the Buchenwald resistance, as well, something that was known to some of the inmates. How it is possible to be in the resistance in a concentration camp I have no idea, but he was. There were approximately 50,000 prisoners at the time. He was put to work as a carpenter and required to produce rabbit cages among other things. He didn't want to help the enemy with their cages, and found better use for the wood. He funneled it to other inmates for use as firewood to cook potatoes they grew in their secret hiding places. That of course meant he had to keep stalling the rabbit cages. When questioned, he continued to think of excuses why he couldn't finish them. When he was finally stuck, and could find no way out, the Americans conveniently came along and bombed the work places in the camp, and with it, whatever he had produced of the rabbit cages. What a wonderful solution to his problem! I guess his guardian angel was looking out for him.

Due to the lack of food, he was entirely emaciated, as were so many. One day, while standing on a scaffold, a guard pushed him, where upon he fell from the scaffold to the ground causing him to break his leg in several places. As no one was to move him, or come to his aid, he was left there to die. However, this dastardly deed saved his life. During the night, inmates from the sick barracks came to move him and they tried fixing him up. For lack of doctors, a professional carpenter set his leg, and repaired it as good as possible. It took many months for him to heal, and his leg was never right again. But because of this, he was eating relatively well and along with the lack of movement, it was the only time in his life my uncle was able to put on weight and was actually heavier than what was in the past.

The inmates had spread rumors that infectious disease was present in the sick barracks. Therefore the Germans, fearing severe illness, would not set foot in there. The inmates managed to save several Jewish children in their barracks by burying them during the day and letting them out at night. A book by Ian Buruma was written about this, entitled *Nude between the Wolves*. The story though true has been quite romanticized and, therefore, lost some of its authenticity.

At the end of 1944, a transport of Jewish women and children arrived in Buchenwald on their way to another camp to be annihilated. My uncle, though not a God-fearing man, prayed that night for the first and last time in his life for God to please end their suffering.

On the evening of April 6, 1945 there were roughly 47,500 inmates in camp Buchenwald, on the Ettersberg Mountain, including 22,900 in the barracks of the main camp and 18,000 housed in the stables of the little camp. On orders from the camp commander, named Pister, the SS had herded another 6,600 Jews for evacuation.

From April 7 to 10, 28,000 from the main and little camps were sent off by rail or driven on foot in the direction of Dachau and Flossenburg camps and the Reissenstadt ghetto. The number of people that died on the evacuation marches can only be roughly estimated, between 12,000 and 15,000. There can't be any doubt that this evacuation was done to kill as many of the already-weakened inmates as possible.

On April 11, a U.S. Army division reached Buchenwald. The SS had fled, but before the army arrived, my Uncle Henk and a Russian man walked to the commanders' office to ask them to surrender. What an unbelievable risk they took, since they did not know the evil men had already flown the coop. Henk and some of the other inmates of the camp's resistance occupied the towers and took charge of order and administration until the Americans could take over. Henk remained in the camp until August, helping out where he could.

He frequently stated that the years in the camp were the best of his life. What he meant was that in the camp everyone was the same. No matter what creed, color, upbringing or disposition they had, everyone fought against the same common enemy, which had created an unprecedented bond. He hoped that this feeling would continue after the war, and was very disappointed when he realized it did not.

He made his way by foot to the south of the Netherlands, where he was asked to be part of a food transport going to the city of Amsterdam. His truck was the only one that made it there. All of the other trucks along the way disappeared, as did the food. The temptation to pilfer the food along the way and sell it on the black market had been too great. He was disgusted to see how quickly they returned to the philosophy of "every man for himself." Knowing of the desperate hunger in Amsterdam, he made sure his truck and its contents made it safely there. As you can tell I loved my uncle Henk, for the things he felt so deeply.

He was married and had a daughter when he was arrested and sent to Buchenwald. When he returned, he found his wife had moved on during his absence, probably thinking he would not come back anyway. The good part is, this left him free to later marry my father's sister, and he became my family. Because of the broken leg that never healed properly; he was paid reparations by the Germans after the war.

On April 16, by order of the American commander, 1,000 citizens of the nearby town of Weimar were forced to tour Buchenwald, where the traces of mass death and horror were still clearly visible. On April 19, there was an international mourning ceremony for the victims of the camp. Survivors took the vow later known as the oath of Buchenwald, to oppose fascism and war. From May to August, some 21,000 liberated survivors left the camp in groups.

Between July 1937 and April 1945, altogether 250,000 people from countries all over Europe were imprisoned in Buchenwald. The number of victims is estimated at approximately 56,000. Of these deaths, 34,375 are registered in the camp's record. The Soviet prisoners of war, who were executed by shooting in the back of the neck, were not registered, nor were the Gestapo inmates—yes there were Gestapo inmates—executed in the Buchenwald crematoriums, estimated at 1,100. Nor were the people who arrived back in Buchenwald on evacuation transports from camps in the east in the spring of 1945, nor the victims of the evacuation marches of April 1945, estimated at 12,000 to 15,000. And remember, this was just one of the concentration camps.

A camp of major significance to Jews in the Netherlands was Westerbork, located a three-hour drive east of Amsterdam, on the German-Dutch border. It was founded in 1939 by the Dutch government to give shelter to German Jews fleeing Nazi persecution. After the occupation of Holland, in a terrible reversal of its saving mission, it became a transit camp through which both Dutch and non-Dutch Jews were transported to concentration camps at Auschwitz, Sobibor, Bergen-Belsen and Theresienstadt, where most were murdered. Gypsies were also deported, and are remembered along with the Jews in the large Appelplatz memorial at Westerbork, designed by a Dutch Jewish Holocaust survivor. It is made of small rectangular stones laid out in patterns on the grounds of the camp. There is one stone for every person who passed through Westerbork—102,000 in total.

Anne Frank became the most famous Dutch girl in WWII for her diary written in hiding in Amsterdam from July 1942 to August 1944. After they were betrayed, the Frank family was transported to Westerbork, where they lived until being deported to Auschwitz in late 1944. Mrs. Frank (Edith) died in Auschwitz. Anne and her sister, Margot, were killed in March 1945 at Bergen-Belsen. Anne was just fifteen. Their father, Otto, had been separated from the family in Auschwitz, and liberated by Soviet Troops in January 1945. After the war he transcribed and published Anne's diary. He died in 1980, having spent the last years of his life in Switzerland, still promoting Anne's message of tolerance and compassion.

It took us years after the war to be able to easily buy clothes. In 1946 my mother had a dress made for me out of a white sheet. The skirt was pleated all around, and since we had no permanent press at the time, it took a full hour to iron it. It was quite a task. Dior's house of fashion developed "The New Look" in 1947. I managed to get one of the new dresses; we did not have to go too far as the store across the street, which had once housed the Jewish bakery, had become a clothing store. They carried all the latest in fashion. I recall standing in line at Roeg's for a shirt for my father as late as 1949.

After the war, upon the arrival of a pastry torte which we later learned would become an annual event, my father told us about the young men he rescued from the train. The boy, whom my father already knew and had saved from the death camps, had become a pastry maker as I mentioned earlier. What happened to the others I do not know, but this one young man had a bakery in Amsterdam and he sent my father a special torte for his birthday, every year, for as long as I can remember. It was a simple and sweet way of showing his gratitude to my father for helping to save his life.

We, as were a lot of European Countries, were greatly helped by the Marshall Plan; this reconstruction plan was established in 1947. It also offered aid to the USSR, but they did not accept it. We rebuilt our bridges, roads and railways that had heavy damage due to flooding and bombardment. It took until well into

1946 before we had our train system running. I hitchhiked out of town to go to the countryside to see friends. I think I would have killed my children if they had done anything so foolish, but there again we take chances when we are very young. Fortunately, I lived to tell about it all.

The American Aid—the Marshall Plan—put us back on our feet, and we gratefully paid off the loan. The Netherlands, as I understand, was one of the few countries to actually repay their loan.

Once the war ended, my mother decided to go to work outside the house; that was a big thing at the time. Not many Dutch housewives held jobs; she was a forerunner. But things were depleted at home as well as everywhere else. She wanted to do this for her family.

She first took a job in an atelier (a French word for a clothing factory) where she was a manager, in Weesp. Eventually, she opened a music store in the seaside town of Zandvoort. She named the shop "RiWi," which stood for Ria and Willem, my parents' first names. When music did not work, she turned it into a store selling beach articles and cosmetics, in the same location. She ran the shop for several years. I used to work there on racing days, days when there were auto races along the beach circuit. I would take the train from home; it took about forty-five minutes to get to Zandvoort from Amsterdam. Race days were extremely busy at the store, and my mother needed my help. I was married by this time and already had three of my four children.

Mom also discovered she had a talent for standup comedy. She performed locally for several organizations to which she belonged, often at holiday time or parties. I still think mom should have been an actress. Performing was something at which she definitely excelled.

Throughout her life, my mother loved and grew red geraniums, the start of which she got from my grandfather. She cut them down every year, and saved the same plants from year to year. I know of several that were well over 50 years old. She passed away in Michigan at age 100. Since her passing, I take red geraniums to her grave every summer.

CHAPTER 22

Pieter's Story

Pieter is a Dutch man I met in Hastings, Michigan, in recent years. Now in his mid 70s, he still suffers from the horrors of the war and his experience in internment camps. I did not know Pieter during the war, but he has become a good friend since. His life is another example of how one person was deprived of his freedom at a very young age. This chapter is his story.

The Dutch East Indies had been our colonies since the sixteen hundreds. There was a large Dutch fleet in the harbor, and many Dutch people had settled around the country with its many islands for generations. Many had never seen the "Motherland." Laws were enforced by Totoks (whites). The East Indies consists of a large number of islands, at the time all governed by the Dutch, and serviced by the shipping company where Pieter's father was an engineer (the Royal Packet and shipping Company) or KPM.

Pieter was born in 1935, in Singapore, the second boy of four. Pieter's parents had met in the Netherlands when his father who ordinarily was working in Jakarta, went on furlough. As these things have a way of happening, he met a lovely girl and had a whirlwind courtship. Though he fell in love while home on furlough and wanted to get married, he had to return to work in Jakarta, Indonesia. Because of job commitments, he could not take time off to return to the Netherlands for his wedding. Just think about that, he could NOT be there for his own wedding. As a result, Bastian and his wife were married by proxy, with his father's brother standing in. This was in the early 1930s, well before the start of WWII. Eventually they did join each other and went on to have four children, all boys, before the war started. Pieter's sister was born in the Netherlands after the war, making the total five.

At one point my dad had been asked if he would be interested in moving to Indonesia, they offered him a post in Jakarta, as a civilian for the Marines, just as he did in Holland, it luckely did not go any further for my mother said NO, just as she later would say NO to emigration to America. Indeed it was lucky, or we too would have ended up in a a Japanese camp, once the Japanese invaded the Islands.

On the morning of January 10, 1942, the Japanese bombed the harbor in Tandjong Priok, Indonesia. It was totally unexpected, just like Pearl Harbor. The carnage was great, and years after the war, sunken ships were still dotting the port. With the help of the Australian fleet, and the Dutch sailors that had escaped Hitler, the battle was fought until March 9, 1942. It too was hopeless, yet they continued the battle for two months, after which the Japanese had the opportunity to invade the country, and the trouble began. Most of the Caucasians had beautiful homes and multiple servants but soon they lost those homes and had to live in internment camps, difficult times for sure.

Indonesians, feeling free after 300 years of Dutch colonial rule, were becoming hostile toward the whites, and posed another threat; they really were in dire straits. I don't think anyone ever foresaw that this would happen.

The Japanese liked to move people in the middle of the night. Pieter recalls how all the women, as well as their children, were under cover of darkness herded onto a train which went nowhere. This happened on several occasions. They had no idea what was going to happen to them. Pieter and his family, as well as many others, were crammed into trucks and taken to their second internment camp. The first camp Pieter remembered as being not too bad. Merchants would come in the morning and as they still had money, they could buy food. However, men and women were separated immediately. As in the Netherlands, resistance sprang up almost immediately. Many men ran and hid in the jungle, where they formed bands of fighters and tried to do what they could to defeat the enemy, not that much different from the underground in Holland.

In Indonesia it was customary and perhaps still is, to transport pigs in small bamboo cages. Men who were caught belonging to the underground were stuffed into such cages. They were, of course, much too small for adult men, which was the first part of their punishment. Once forced into the cages, the men were left outside in the searing hot tropical sun for several days, deprived of food and water, while the guards stood nearby taunting them by drinking and even spilling the leftover water on the ground. After several days like that, the cages were loaded on trucks, taken to a port, loaded onto a boat, and dumped in the sea. It is hard to imagine such cruelty.

For more than three years, Pieter's family had no idea what had happened to their father. Pieter's mother was alone with her boys. During those years, they received no education. Pieter had just started first grade when they were sent to the camp. There were no books to read. His mother had brought her Bible, the New Testament, and tried to give the kids reading lessons with that. Later, after the war's end, they had to attend a special school to help them bridge the lack of several years of education.

Subsequent camps were much worse. At the first one, they had some semblance of their own life; they lived without other families. When the Japanese decided they needed to be moved again, in the middle of the night, they were all herded onto a train headed for another camp. This camp had huts made of bamboo, with coconut palm roofs and dirt floors. They were surrounded by two rows of fences this time. For the next few years, there was no place to go and guards were everywhere. News trickled into Holland about the extreme hunger, and the cruelties the Japanese guards were performing.

The prisoners were given one bowl of rice and some sort of watery vegetable soup per day. Some of the women complained about the rationing of the food. As punishment, the Japanese shaved one side of their heads bald and then paraded them around to show the other prisoners, and let everyone see who was boss. The next day they repeated the act on the other side of their heads, and they were paraded again.

Then a directive from the captors came and for three days there was no food for anyone. Pieter remembers picking bread out of garbage cans, and going to the ovens to scrape out the crust that was left there. They were desperate for food; anything to eat. In a fight for survival, Pieter's mother sold her diamond wedding ring to the Japanese for food, and the soldiers gladly supplied. Unfortunately, she had only one valuable to offer and the food did not last very long, so they continued to starve along with the others. Sadly, twin girls in the hut next to them died. Their mother was inconsolable, and wanted to die as well. As a parent myself, I can understand her feelings.

At the last camp, Pieter, then age nine, crawled through a drain pipe, to go underneath the fences to catch large frogs. One time the guard heard him. Pieter, in his youthful bravado, tried to hit the guard, whose head stuck out above the fence, with a stick. Taunted, the guard stuck his bayonet through the fence, but luckily did not harm him. Pieter returned home with frogs, where they removed the heads, took out the yellow fat, and fried it in that fat for dinner. One will eat almost anything when hungry enough.

Meanwhile, Pieter's brother, Kees, had celebrated his eleventh birthday. As with all boys, once they reached the age of eleven, he was taken out of the camp. During the remainder of the war, his mother had no idea where he was, or even if he was alive. They later learned that he had been in a camp, Bogor, adjacent to the one in which his father was imprisoned. So while they were both imprisoned within a mile of each other, they had no idea. What a comfort it would have been had they each known that each other was still alive.

In the camps they had to share sleeping quarters with women and children. They slept on down sloping wooden benches; the high part served as pillow, while at the low part one's feet often touched—and rested against—the feet of other sleepers. There was some sort of a bridge in the center, but nonetheless, it was tight quarters for all. I do not know about toilet facilities, but I have a hunch they were not in great supply either.

When the Japanese capitulated, the Allied planes came to make food drops. Now the Japanese had left, they could feel the hostility towards the colonials sharply increase. The former prisoners were taken by bus to Campoeng Makasar, which was another camp with glass shards on the top of the fence, where the Dutch were protected by Gurkas and Sikhs (religious sects from India), Hi Ho's, against the hostility of the Indonesian people. It was thought that there would be a massacre of the Dutch, without the added protection. In Indonesia, as in the Netherlands, there was an underground movement that attempted to fight the uprising. This was supported with troops sent in from the Netherlands. The Indonesians wanted to be free at any cost, and the Netherlands finally agreed it was time to hand over power. It was sometime in 1946 when Pieter and his family returned to the Netherlands.

As mentioned, there had been no formal schooling during the years in the camp. There were many other Dutch children who also had been in the Japanese camps in the same position as Pieter. Although then eleven years old, he had to go back to basics to catch up on his education. Transitional arrangements were made for all such children returning from the camps in Indonesia.

Pieter returned to Indonesia again, at age seventeen, but was unable to adjust to life as it was at that time. He returned to Holland once again, but did not feel it was home anymore either. He then applied for immigration to Australia. Once there, he became a soldier in the Australian service. While in Australia, he married a Dutch girl and had a daughter. When his wife was twenty-seven years old, she was killed in a car accident. That ended his military career, and again he returned to Holland, where at least he had family who could help him with raising his daughter, who was only six years old at the time her mother was killed. When his daughter was seventeen, he decided to study in America to become a pilot. The intention was that he would study a year, go back home and fly. He learned too late that this was not possible because the license he obtained in the U.S. was not valid in the Netherlands.

Unfortunately for him his daughter was not interested in going with him to America. Well, she was seventeen and that is the way it goes when you are seventeen. There are boyfriends, and then of course there was school. As a result, Pieter came to American for study alone, and the plan to go back in a year fell flat on its face because, as I mentioned, his license was not valid overseas. He remained in the U.S. and taught flying for many years and still renews his license every two years. The experience of the internment camps and other horrors of the war have never left him.

CHAPTER 23

The Big Picture

In the end, "The Great War"—World War I—was dwarfed by World War II. It had become the largest and most violent armed conflict in the history of mankind, both in terms of human and material resources expended. In all, sixty-one countries with 1.7 billion people—three-fourths of the world's population—were involved in one way or another.

Most statistics on the war are only estimates. Its vastness and chaotic sweep made uniform record keeping impossible. Some governments lost control of the data, and some resorted to manipulating it for political reasons.

A rough consensus has been reached on the total cost of the war. In terms of money spent, it has been put at more than $1 trillion, which makes it more expensive than all other wars combined, up to that point in time. The United States alone spent an estimated $341 billion ($50 billion in Lend-Lease payments). Next, in order: Germany, $272 billion; USSR, $192 billion; Britain, $120 billion; Italy, $94 billion; and Japan, $56 billion. Beyond the cost of the war, the USSR lost thirty percent of its national wealth. Total empires were lost.

Property damage and looting were of incalculable amounts for occupied countries like the Netherlands. And Germany was not spared. Bombing and shelling there had produced over four billion cubic meters of shrapnel and rubble. A German musician I hosted in Michigan in the early 1990s, then in his early fifties, recalled that when he was a young child he thought the whole world looked like that—nothing but rubble. It was all he could see, wherever he looked.

A total of 110 million persons were mobilized for military service, the top three being the USSR (34 million), the United States (16 million) and Germany (9 million).

The human cost, not including more than six million indirect victims—the Jews killed in the Holocaust—is estimated to have been fifty-five million dead. That included forty-four million of the Allies and eleven million for the Axis. Of the fifty-five million dead, twenty-five million were in the military and thirty million were civilians.

Military deaths for the Allies are estimated at nineteen million in Europe, and six million in the war with Japan. Figures for major Allied countries are: USSR 11,285,000; China 1,400,000 (Japanese front), Britain 305,800; Yugoslavia 300,000; U.S. 290,000; France 122,000; Poland 110,800. Military deaths for major Axis countries were roughly eleven million, among them: Germany 3,250,000; Japan 1,740,000; Romania 540,000; Hungary 136,000; and Italy 226,900.

On the civilian side, death numbers are equally staggering. Major Allied losses are estimated at: USSR, 16 million; China, 10 million (Japanese front); Yugoslavia, 1,400,000; Greece, 415,000; Czechoslovakia 215,000. Poland lost 5.4 million civilians, about thirty percent of its population, the most of any country. This was mainly because Poland had a significantly large number of Jews, targeted for elimination by the Nazis.

The same source estimated Dutch military deaths at 13,700 and civilian deaths at 150,000. That very rough estimate probably does not take into account the many that died later as a result of their time in the camps. My Uncle Max lived only eleven months after his release in 1946; he was very sick and malnourished when he came home.

The Netherlands, Amsterdam in particular, was a major Jewish population center in the hundred years leading up to World War II. In 1939, there were roughly 140,000 Jews living in the Netherlands; about 90,000 in Amsterdam. In 1945, only about 35,000 of the 140,000 were still alive. Many were reportedly rounded up, arrested and deported at the hands of Dutch Nazi sympathizers. However, the Dutch underground is estimated to have hidden 25,000 to 30,000 Jews, many of whom survived. After the war, many surviving Jews immigrated to Israel, still home to some 6,000 Dutch Jews. Today there are an estimated 45,000 Jews in the Netherlands, almost half of them living in Amsterdam.

Of course, not only the Jews suffered. World War II has a lasting influence on all of Dutch society. May 4 is a national day of commemorating those who died during the war. And among the living there are many—both in my parents' generation and my own—who still have emotional problems relating to the war. The day has such strong emotions that when I was about to give birth to my eldest son, my husband wanted me to wait a day rather than have the child on May 4. May 5 was a day of joy. Needless to say he would not wait; my son Roy's birthday is May 4.

In addition to lives lost and monetary expense, the world balance of power was also affected by World War II. When it was over, Britain, France, Germany and Japan were no longer great military powers. Only two were left. The USSR was strong in much of Eastern Europe, and the United States had become the world's strongest military, economic and political power. It had also ushered in the nuclear age.

Not everything was negative. American wartime developments in science and technology provided new tools for the solution of pre-war problems that had been put aside, and solved new war-related problems as well. During the war, many inventions were being made, such as jet engines, tape recorders, radar, microwaves, nuclear power, and ball-point pens, just to name a few, and let's not forget penicillin. World War II was one of history's most powerful catalysts for change.

At the close of the war, leaders of the main victors—Roosevelt from the U.S., Stalin from the Soviet Union, and Churchill from Britain—formed the United Nations to replace the old League of Nations started by President Woodrow Wilson. Fifty-one countries signed the charter. Today there are 192 member states, representing virtually every recognized independent state in the world. Its goal was to intervene in conflicts between nations and thereby avoid war. It has its critics, and has by no means ended all war, but at least there has not been a third world war.

After the war, Johnny Roeg reopened his parents' dry goods store, and ran it for as long as I can remember. He must have sold it later for I remember returning home for a visit and seeing a toy store in its place. The older Nicky Roeg owned a bar in Amsterdam. His son Nicky, the younger boy I knew, must be in his late sixties by now. There is a film producer named Nicolas Roeg who lives in England. I have often wondered if he could be one of the Roegs' relatives. I have tried to contact him, but to no avail.

Epilogue

We survived the war, as well as everyone in our extended family. We bucked up, and made the best of it. After the war, my father had "wanderlust," and the Netherlands felt too small for him. Because he had been a political prisoner, he was offered emigration to America in 1957. He accepted, and three months after the World Council of Churches agreed to sponsor him, he and my two brothers moved to Grand Rapids, Michigan. My mother would not follow them to America to live, although she made many visits to Michigan, frequently for six months at a time.

I had married and was raising a family when my father and brothers left for America; and we remained in the Netherlands for three more years. It was around Christmas of 1959 that my husband and I, with our three children, immigrated to Grand Rapids, Michigan. I promptly became pregnant, for a total of four children—three Dutch and one American. I had two girls and two boys, just right. Life is difficult for an immigrant; you stay with one foot in your own language and culture. I walked in two worlds for many years, and still yearn for Europe when I see a movie that is shot there, even though I like America and now consider it home.

My sister also eventually moved to the United States. My mother remained a resident of the Netherlands, although she continued to visit us here right up to the end of her long life. I still live in Michigan, having made many visits to my homeland and neighboring parts of Europe over the years. In May 2007, I took my oath and am now an American citizen.

My father eventually returned to the Netherlands, at age sixty-three. There, he lived out his remaining years in Amsterdam, and died of old age at eighty-three. Now that I have entrusted my memories to paper, I wonder if I have given my father all the credit he so rightly deserved, for taking all the chances he took, and all of the things he did to keep us alive, all of which I simply took for granted at the time. Heroism requires taking risks. My father was a hero, as was my mother, each in their own unique way.

I have said that wartime in the Netherlands left an indelible imprint on my life. Some things are easy to identify. I could not become a ballerina, because one must do it when in one's prime; and my chance had passed by the time the war ended. There are foods I will never again eat. I cannot be around fireworks, as the sound makes me relive the bombs of war.

Other things are more subjective. I am pleased that I have not let the war experiences make me bitter. In fact, I believe I am more compassionate. In part, this has come from experiences later in life, for the Germans remained the enemy to me until the 1990s.

It took me until the early 1990s, when hosting a group of German musicians in Michigan, to realize that the German civilians had suffered, too. One of them told me, "I begged my mother to let me sleep in my own bed instead of in an air raid shelter." She lived in Aachen, close to the Dutch border. No doubt, as in my own country, the air raid sirens would wail when the planes entered the border area, and for them the search lights would crisscross the sky as well.

I learned the Allied soldiers were not blameless; the last fourteen days before the war ended, an Allied pilot flew over a small town in Germany every day, and shot at every living thing he saw, animal and human.

In 1995, I hosted a group of German musicians again, and befriended the couple I was hosting. My friend has no fingers on one hand except his pinky finger. As a child in Germany he had picked up a shiny object in the road near his home, and it blew his fingers off as well as blinded him in one eye. War is hard on everyone.

During the 1990s, I went to Margraven Cemetery in the Southern part of the Netherlands, where more than eight thousand of our men are buried. As I stood there I cried, as I did again while I was writing this book. There were endless rows of crosses. I ran my fingers over the wall with some of the Michiganders' names; that is all I could do for them.

Many years later, I learned that my family originated in Denmark. Prior to 1500, they had traveled to Germany, where they remained for several hundred years. My branch of the family left Germany in 1706 and went to Amsterdam, because all of the towns in which they lived had become Catholic and they were Protestant. We could have been killing our own distant relatives during the war; or, even scarier to think is that we could have been on the German side of this atrocious period of ruthless killing.

While on a trip to Germany, in 1995, I discovered a distant relative. I had traveled from Amsterdam with a German musician friend, Narthan, who had stayed with my girlfriend when we hosted foreign bands through Blue Lake Arts Camp.

My cousin Tim had given me a copy of our family tree that he had researched from the time the family had come to The Netherlands, but had stated that the family had lived in Geseke and Paderborn, in addition to Lippstadt. At one time, our name was then Modersohn von Lippstadt.

As I recounted this to Narthan, he exclaimed that he also had family from Geseke. He said he would be happy to take me to Paderborn, but not Lippstadt, as it was too far away. And so we set out for his house in Germany. Meanwhile, we had the radio on in the car. They announced that there had been an accident on the Autobahn, so Narthan pulled off the next exit. Otherwise, we knew it could be a long wait until the accident was cleared from the roads. Almost immediately as we pulled off the freeway, I realized we were in Lippstadt. Imagine my surprise when I suddenly found myself there. The section we were in was the downtown area. We came upon a Protestant church. It was stone and had been built in the 1200s. We decided to stop and enter. As soon as I stepped into the church, which dated 1208, I knew that my so very distant family must have been members there at one time. It was the most extreme and uncanny feeling I have ever had; I felt I was supposed to be there.

146

The Modersohn Family Crest.

The church was empty when we entered. There was an organ inside. Narthan suggested I be seated and he would play for me. What I thought was an organ was actually a glockenspiel. As it was around 7:00 p.m. when Narthan began to play, the glockenspiel started the bells chiming—at anything but their usual times. This sound, of course, attracted a church elder who came to see what was going on in the church. He introduced himself as Herr Müeller.

We were caught off guard, and so, as sort of an excuse for us being in the church at night, Narthan told the man that I was a Moederzoon from Lippstadt, living in Amsterdam, looking for a relative by the name of Modersohn. The church elder looked at Narthan and me and said, "I worked for him for forty years." So unbelievable to both Narthan and I, this had to be a miracle. Lippstadt is a town of 72,000 people and thus not a small village. So here we have the same name in three different languages: Morsonne, from Denmark where we originated; Modersohn, the German version; and Moederzoon, the Dutch spelling, but all with the same meaning which is mother's son.

Meanwhile, I wanted to take some pictures of this very old church but my camera was still in Narthan's car. Narthan gave his business card to Herr Müeller, stating that if Herr Modersohn was interested to meet his distant relative, to please have him give us a call. Narthan then went to get my camera from his car, but it seemed that he inadvertently picked up the church keys, thinking they were his car keys, and put them in his coat pocket.

The next morning we were ready to go sightseeing, specifically castles, as I adore castles. Narthan reached into his pocket for his car keys and out came the keys to the church! It happened to be on a Saturday morning. The only two names in Lippstadt we knew were Herr Müeller and Modersohn. Narthan called information to obtain Herr Müeller's phone number.

As it turns out, there was no listing for Herr Müeller. Narthan then asked for Herr Modersohn. This time we struck gold. After ringing the number, my distant cousin came to the phone and spoke to Narthan, who told him not only about the church keys but also about the events at the church the prior day. We learned then that Ernst Modersohn had been waiting for years to get to know one of the Dutch Moederzoons. He had been aware of the split in the family when the protestant group of relatives left for Amsterdam.

Ernst asked Narthan to please come back to Lippstadt that afternoon around 4 p.m. He gave us his home address. It was over a two-hour drive from where we were, but we had to return the church keys. I cannot say that I wasn't excited at the prospective thought of meeting a distant relative; even though it was disappointing to miss out on the castles we had planned to see. Returning the keys was at the top of the list as well, so Narthan and I got on the autobahn once again, where he drove us back to Lippstadt. This proved to be a very scary situation, because my friend drove like a maniac, for which he later got scolded by his wife.

When we arrived in Lippstadt, Ernst was not at home. His wife, Gerda, came to the door and welcomed us inside. Imagine my surprise when I saw the coffee table. It was a setting fit for royalty, with a wonderful spread of bonbons, liqueurs, and all kinds of pastries, all in our honor. A few minutes after we arrived, Ernst came home. I was speechless to see how much he resembled our family. My first words to him were, "Oh, my God, you look so much like my father and even more so my uncle." We certainly have strong family genes. Think about that, we had left that country 300 years earlier.

Through Ernst I learned that there were still many Modersohns living in Germany, as well as thousands in Denmark. Ernst gave me a family tree, dating back to 1543. It was also the first time I laid eyes on the Moederzoon family crest, which was printed on the paper, alongside the family tree.

I had no idea that the reason he was not at home when we arrived was because he was out getting a copy of our combined family tree. It had been drawn by a professor at the University of Berlin, who was, you guessed it, a Modersohn with the first name of Fritz. Narthan and I spent a delightful afternoon with Ernst and Gerda, talking, sharing stories, and laughing. Narthan, a German, translated for me—the kid who had refused to learn the language—during our first meeting. Their hospitality was unforgettable. I was invited to come back at any time.

As I am writing this I am listening to the bells of Lippstadt, a small gift from Ernst and Gerda.

In 1998, I returned to Lippstadt. This time, Gerda did the translating, as she spoke English; Ernst did not. We kept in touch for years after our first meeting. They wanted me to come back again, after their 60th wedding anniversary, but I never heard from them again. They were approaching their 70s when we met. I have no idea if they had taken ill and/or passed away, but it is a memory I cannot forget. It is also such a simple but powerful reminder that we all are so connected in many ways. Ernst's brother died during the war, as did Gerda's. I do have relatives in Denmark, as well as in Germany; though I have not met them, we are still from the same family tree. Wars do no good; rather they serve to pit relatives—no matter how distant—against one another.

We , people in general, are social animals, klinging to family and friends. I share my DNA with thousands, as all of you do, and yet throughout history we continue with our inhumanity towards each other.

I believe in Peace

REFERENCES

Barbour, John. "German Invasion Seemed Unbeatable, but Dunkirk Escape
Gave Allies Hope." *The Grand Rapids Press*. (Grand Rapids, MI). 6 May 1990.

Barbour, John. "Remembering the Day Poland was Invaded." *The Grand Rapids Press*. (Grand Rapids, MI). May 1990.

Breuer, William. *Top Secret Tales of World War II*. John Wiley & Sons, 2000.

Churchill, Winston S. *The Second World War—Closing the Ring*. Boston: Houghton Mifflin Company, 1951.

Dekker, Maurits. *De Laars op de Nek 1939-1944 (With the Boot on the Neck)*. Leiden: A.W. Sijthoff, 1960.

Hoekstra, Han G. and Evert Werkman. *Nee an Nog Eens Nee—Fotobook van het Verzet, 1940-1945 (No, No, and No Again—a Photobook of the Resistance)*. Amsterdam: N.V. Het Parool, 1965.

Ryan, Cornelius. *A Bridge Too Far*. New York: Simon and Schuster, 1974. Maps by Rafael Palacios, inside covers and pp. 56-57.

Speijers, Nolly. "Operatie Market Garden—September 1944." *De Telegraaf* (Amsterdam, The Netherlands). 11 Sep. 2004.

To further explore topics researched on the Internet, visit:
Answers.com/World War II
Answers.com/Bailey Bridge
Answers.com/21st Army Group
BBC.co.uk/history/worldwars/wwtwo/battle_arnhem
Cympm.com/judenrat.html
Geocities.com/pentagon/world war II
GoDutch.com/windmill/newsitem.asp?id=291 (Battle of Overloon)

Grolier.com/wwii/wwii4.html (Fall of the Low Countries)

Historyonthenet.com /WW2/WW2_timeline.htm

Holland.com/uk/special_battlefields/overloon.html

JewishGeneralorg/Forgottencamps/Camps/General/Liste
    Eng.html

JewishGeneralorg/Forgottencamps/Camps/BuchenwaldEng.
    html

JewishGeneralorg/Forgottencamps/Camps/VughtEng.html

Jhm.nl/amsterdam_eng.aspx?ID=39 (Asscher Diamond
    Factory)

MarketGarden.com/2010/UK/frames.html

Stonebooks.com/archives/040822.shtml (The Great Mis-
    take by Peter Beale)

Chgs.umn.edu/visual__Artistic_resources/Public_Holo-
    caust_Memorials/Westerbork_Concentration_Camp/
    westerbork_concentration_camp.html

WorldAtlas.com/webimage/countrys/europe/nl.htm

Worldwar2database.com/html/Ardennes.htm

Worldwar2database.com/html/Arnhem.htm

Special acknowledgment to the Wikipedia Foundation,
    licensed to the public under the terms of the GNU Free
    Documentation License.

Reference http://en.Wikipedia.org.wiki/ on the following
topics:
    Antwerp
    Arnhem
    Asscher_Brothers
    Battle_of_Overloon
    Battle_of_the_Scheldt
    History_of_Jews_in_the_Netherlands
    Les_Gueux
    Netherlands_in World_War_II
    Operation_Market-Garden
    United_Nations
    Vught
    Western_Front_World_War_II

CPSIA information can be obtained
at www.ICGtesting.com
Printed in the USA
BVHW091624150920
588719BV00006B/502